The

HOSPITALITY AND LEISURE
ARCHITECTURE

of

WIMBERLY ALLISON TONG & GOO

AIR MAIL
PAR AVION

ADMITTED
U. S. CUSTOMS
U. S. IMMIGRATION
JFK AIRPORT

ROCKPORT
PUBLISHERS

Rockport Publishers
Rockport, Massachusetts

First published in the United States of America by:
Rockport Publishers, Inc.
146 Granite Street
Rockport, Massachusetts 01966
Telephone: (508) 546-9590
Fax: (508) 546-7141

ISBN 1-56496-140-0

10 9 8 7 6 5 4 3 2 1

Created by:
Howard J. Wolff
Art Direction and Design:
Laura P. Herrmann

Cover Photographs:
Front Cover
Hotel Bora Bora, Douglas Peebles
The Palace of The Lost City, Courtesy of Sun International
Back Cover
Disney's© Grand Floridian Beach Resort, Courtesy of Disney Development Company
The Ritz-Carlton, Laguna Niguel, Milroy & McAleer
Hyatt Regency Kauai, Milroy & McAleer
Stamp Collage Artist:
Stephen M. Boss

Printed in Hong Kong

ACKNOWLEDGEMENTS

by Donald W.Y. Goo, FAIA
WAT&G Chairman of the Board

HOSPITALITY AND LEISURE DESIGN attracts many to its doors; this is an architecture that is as gracious to groups as it is to individuals.

Similarly, our thanks go to groups of people as well as to individuals:

To WAT&G clients, who honor us by assigning their dreams to our drawing boards.

To WAT&G staff, who work tirelessly to delight people they will never see.

Of all the individuals to thank, Howard Wolff deserves special acknowledgement as this book's architect.

The contributions of Ray Bradbury, John Naisbitt, and Mike Rubin are extraordinary, especially in light of their renown and the fullness of their individual schedules. Mazeppa King Costa, Beth Crawford Vincent, and Jana Wolff — three fine writers who contributed the lion's share of the chapters — have told the WAT&G story with as much beauty and clarity as the architecture itself.

Spending hours behind photo lenses and lupes were photography coordinators Olivier Koning and David Lindsay. And the project would never have been realized without Jan Stenberg, Leilani Fortuno, Amy Stillman, Cindy Wasserman, Mark Tawara, Justin Henderson, David Huffman, Emily Pagliaro, and Elena Lau, whose efforts are directly responsible for this book.

Last and first thanks go to Rockport Publishers and to Rosalie Grattaroti, who thought ours was a story you might like to read; Shawna Mullen, the book's editor; and Laura Herrmann, graphic designer.

TABLE OF CONTENTS

PREFACE

by the principals of
Wimberly Allison Tong & Goo

THE CHARACTER OF A FIRM evolves over time. Being approached by Rockport Publishers to tell the WAT&G story is a delightful reason to pause and reflect on who we are: where we've come from, where we're headed, and what makes us different. That's no small task when you consider that we're over 200 individuals working from 4 separate offices on projects in 50 countries.

As we look back over the last five decades, distinctive patterns emerge. In the work we produce and in the process of working, we have always tried to make a positive contribution to people and places around the world. The success of our projects — in fact, the success of our firm — depends on how well we've listened to the people and to the places that are hosts to our designs.

"YOU WANT TO FEEL LIKE YOU ARE THERE WHEN YOU ARE THERE."

In a word, our projects belong. Many of our projects start out with WAT&G team members living on site to get a feeling for the land. Concepts are much more real when an architect is standing on a bluff than when sitting in a conference room miles away.

As architects and planners, we recognize that we have an opportunity — and more than that, a responsibility — to preserve and enhance the very qualities that give a place its special character. Imposing ideas from outside doesn't work. What does work is immersion in the culture of a specific place, allowing that culture to give its time-tested answers to particular questions regarding appropriate design.

Long before it was fashionable, George J. "Pete" Wimberly was creating architecture with a strong sense of place. Soon after he founded the architectural firm in Hawaii in

1945, Pete was commissioned to be the resident architect for the rebuilding of the Royal Hawaiian — one of only two hotels in Waikiki at the time. Even then, Pete felt it was incumbent on him and his partners to provide an architecture that was expressive of the Hawaiian culture. WAT&G went on to create hundreds of successful projects over the next five decades, all the while heeding the principle of cultural authenticity.

"IF YOU WANT TO WORK IN ONE PLACE, YOU GENERALIZE; IF YOU WANT TO WORK EVERYWHERE, YOU SPECIALIZE."

We made a choice early on. The choice to become specialists in tourism-related projects went against the prevailing custom of most architects to avoid being narrowly defined. But WAT&G continued to cultivate its expertise in hotels and resorts, sensing an expanding interest in travel to foreign lands. We also came to recognize that the complexity of the hospitality industry demands specialization. There is hardly a project more complex than a destination resort, which embodies all of the same elements as a small city.

The potential drawbacks of specialization — the emergence of stereotypical buildings and boredom among the architects who work on them — have been avoided by our insistence that buildings reflect the forms, details, and qualities of the land on which they sit. We have no signature style; our hallmark is our versatility — the ability to design for different themes, scales, and settings. Suggest that WAT&G is eclectic in its design styles, and we will take it as a compliment.

Half a century later, our early decision to specialize has served us well — positioning

WAT&G as an international leader in our industry and bringing to our clients the benefits of accumulated experience and expertise.

Of course, none of our work would be possible without the vision and knowledge of clients who understand what people want and how to give it to them — clients who continually strive to balance environmental sensitivity and business sensibility.

It is through these years of specialization that we have gained an intimate knowledge of the business and operations behind a hotel or resort. We care just as much about how a building works as how it looks. We want our designs to please people and, at the same time, to function profitably (thereby pleasing certain other people).

"THE VALUE OF GOOD DESIGN – WHAT THE BUILDING LOOKS LIKE AND HOW IT FEELS TO PEOPLE – CAN BE RUNG UP ON A CASH REGISTER."

Buildings that beckon guests to return again and again make money for their owners. They are profitable not only because they satisfy guests, but also because they satisfy the people who work there. Facilities that are well designed, both in public areas and behind the scenes, can serve to attract qualified staff, enhance morale, and even increase productivity. In an industry like travel and tourism, where high staff turnover is a universal concern, architecture can make a measurable difference.

Architects are part of a much larger group of professionals whose combined efforts are required to create a successful development. WAT&G architects are always part of a team and are often in the role of team leader, orchestrating as many as 5,000 team members, including construction workers, artisans, and armies of special design consultants.

"YOU HAVE TO BE TWO THINGS TO WORK AROUND THE WORLD – NIMBLE ENOUGH TO GO WHERE THE ACTION IS AND HUMBLE ENOUGH TO LISTEN ONCE YOU GET THERE."

On WAT&G projects around the world, we actively seek out local architectural firms for collaboration. Many of the projects featured in this book were completed in association with colleagues from other countries.

Different cultures, different time zones, different languages and technologies: these are all a part of our everyday work. On the day these words are being written, we have WAT&G staff members working miles from home in locations as far apart as Vanuatu in the Pacific Islands; Ankor Wat, Cambodia; Johor Bahru, Malaysia; Amman, Jordan; Eilat, Israel; Ixtapa, Mexico; San Andres, Colombia; Las Vegas, Nevada; and Windsor, England.

To be where clients need us, we log 256,850 miles in an average month. The geographic reach of our practice is a good match for the multicultural staff that comprises WAT&G. All together, we represent 21 nationalities and speak 27 languages!

"DESTINATIONS ARE SHAPED BY THE QUEST OF THE TRAVELER. AND THE QUEST OF TODAY'S TRAVELER IS CHANGING RAPIDLY."

From our roots in hotels and resorts, our portfolio of projects has expanded over the years as the marketplace has enlarged its definition of hospitality and leisure. In the pages that follow, you will find examples of hotels, theme parks, health spas, golf clubhouses, family entertainment centers, marinas, beach clubs, casinos, timeshare condominiums, and even a quarter-mile-long, 20-deck cruise ship.

At a particularly exciting time in history, we are part of the largest industry in the world — travel and tourism. Popular new technologies in the leisure and entertainment fields suggest that you can experience a place without visiting it; we maintain that people will continue to want to travel, continue to want the *real thing*.

As travelers seek new adventures and discover new destinations, we want to help them celebrate the people and the traditions that make each place special.

GLOBALIZATION OF THE WORLD'S LARGEST INDUSTRY

by John Naisbitt

THE WORLD'S LARGEST INDUSTRY — travel and tourism — is driven as no other by individuals' decisions. The smallest players decide. This situation also reflects a global paradox: the more universal we become, the more tribal we act. The bigger and more competitive travel becomes, the more authentically distinctive to tourists we will make our cultures.

The more we integrate the world, the more we differentiate our experiences. The more exposure we have to other cultures, languages, and landscapes, the stronger our desire to experience them firsthand.

The growing expectations of the experienced traveler for all things cultural, exotic, and untrammeled by fellow tourists have created enormous demand for specialty trips and tours. The industry has responded: cultural tourism and ecotourism are two rapidly growing segments of the travel industry.

A growing number of countries are recognizing that the world's appetite for experiencing environments and cultures other than their own presents a golden economic opportunity. Tourists bring with them a ready supply of foreign currency and a taste for all things representative of local culture. As areas become increasingly popular international travel destinations, they also become attractive investment opportunities for multinational developers of hotels, theme parks, special events coordinators, and resort communities. In this way, tourism is a self-perpetuating industry.

In the 21st century there will be few barriers to international travel. Tourists will be courted by Third World and developed countries alike for the enormous infusion of capital that accompanies tourism, and for the benefits realized from a heightened awareness and appreciation of global cultural diversity.

Already a global industry by virtue of the sheer number of people traveling internationally, by cooperative arrangements between international air carriers, and by foreign investments in hotels and tourist attractions, it will become increasingly so. Deregulation of the airline industries in every country will be followed by more liberal policies on foreign investment in all travel and travel-related industries.

Tourism is the force that will make the global village truly one world.

These trends have found their way into the architecture of Wimberly Allison Tong & Goo. The essential quality of the firm's work — the creation of a sense of place — holds the key to what travelers are looking for when they get there...wherever *there* is.

9

THE ANATOMY OF A DESTINATION

by Michael S. Rubin, Ph.D.

THE LONGING FOR LEISURE

According to Aristotle, the highest purpose of a civilization was to create meaningful forms of leisure for its citizens — and for the individual the ideal to be sought was leisure as an exploration of the good life. Leisure as it was first defined during that Golden Age was the ultimate destination and a necessity for the development and renewal of a democratic society.

Despite 20 centuries of astonishing technological development, western civilization has lost much of the insight and ideals of the ancient Greeks. Today most of our leisure time is given over to amusements, to a hiatus from the work-a-day world. Yet the longing for the good life, for personal renewal, for enrichment and discovery, has never been greater. In an age in which every place is electronically accessible but remote from our touch, we seek remote places which offer access to new perspectives, discoveries, and encounters.

THE CREATION OF A DESTINATION

The destination is first and foremost an imagined place, an ideal experience we hope for in the future and cherish from the past. As an ideal place, the destination cannot simply be appreciated passively but requires participation in an experience which is, by definition, transitory. Physically and psychologically the guest must leave a familiar world of routines to enter a novel realm of discovery and renewal. It is inevitable that the guest will eventually return to that world, but with the possibility that the place visited will provide a transformative experience. More often than not, it is the promise of renewal that summons a return to a special place, remembered during the height of

occupational activity as the beginning of a preferred destiny.

Creating a destination, a setting for leisure and renewal, is therefore a special kind of place making. The destination as derived from its Latin root *destinare* represents both a journey and a promise, the belief that there is both a rhyme (poetic) and reason (noetic) to one's life. The destination is at once the portal, way station, and terminus of a hopeful journey toward renewal, re-creation, and transformation.

For half a century, Wimberly Allison Tong & Goo has been on the leading edge of destination architecture. This is not simply because the firm has designed more resorts and leisure centers than any other firm — quantity must take a back seat to quality in the architecture of destinations. Nor is it due to the fact that the firm has specialized in hospitality and leisure projects — after all, destination architecture relates to all manner of transformative places, from the church to the symphony hall. It is that WAT&G, over the past 50 years, has developed an architectural language that infuses destinations with a promise of transformation for their visitors.

Destination architecture combines the architectonics of a place, a journey, and a dream. To reveal this hidden structure requires a framework for understanding the visitor's experience, beginning with the contemplation of a visit, followed by the experience itself, and concluding with the recollection of the treasured place.

THE IMAGERY OF A DISTANT PLACE

Any journey begins with the hope for fulfillment that might be provided by a special place, distinct and distant from the familiar

surroundings of the everyday world. These places are not necessarily far away geographically, but must provide the imagery of a distant place. Long before the arrival experience, the expectant visitor pores over travel books, maps, and brochures. The implicit search is for an image that connotes what one believes can be found in this distant place — through its culture, nature, or history.

The image of a distant place is captured nowhere more convincingly than in the Hotel Bora Bora. One first sees a village of traditional Tahitian *farés*, perched along a reef of the Bora Bora Lagoon, and then realizes that this idyllic Polynesian village is a hotel. The exotic essence of Tahiti, the spirit that nurtured Gauguin, is promised in an image that did not exist on this paradisal setting before 1969. The architectonics of the destination begins with the articulation of the traveler's aspiration — the hope of entering another realm.

THE EXPERIENCE OF A TRANSITORY PLACE

Neither the dream of a far-off place nor the journey to the destination ends with the traveler's long awaited arrival, for what is most unique about the destination place is its transitory nature. It is within this context that the destination is transformed from an image into a place. Remarkably, it is the transitory nature of the visit that provides the structure for place making. The architectonics of the destination involves an orchestrated sequence of transitional settings that provide a framework in which the visitor is offered the opportunity to enter a realm removed from the temper of everyday life. Several elements serve to define this transitional structure.

ARRIVAL: SETTINGS AND STRUCTURE

The transition experience begins at the point of arrival. Arrival further articulates the image of the resort by providing a distinctive setting for making the transition from anonymous traveler to honored guest. There is also a structure to arrival that must be carefully designed, which includes the efficient movement of thousands of visitors, tons of luggage, hundreds of vehicles, and myriad behind-the-scenes services.

At the Hyatt Regency Kauai, the arrival setting conveys a sense of the traditional Hawaiian welcome, involving an intimacy between host and guest in which the *hale* (or house) is made fully accessible. To achieve this effect, WAT&G turned back to the classic Hawaiian resort architecture of the 1930s as well as traditional plantation houses.

The guest receives a ceremonial welcome upon arrival at the hotel's porte cochere and is greeted by a sequence of open-air courts and sheltered enclaves. An open court provides a view across to a lively social space and out to the blue expanse of the Pacific. Indigenous woods, woven *lau hala* wall coverings, and grillwork designed to portray Kauai's native plants create the sense of entering a home adorned with the treasures and heirlooms of many generations.

Check-in occurs when the guest is ready to partake of this minor formality. Transitions from the entry lobby are marked by open portals, subtle changes in decoration and furnishings, and shifts in elevation. A separate entrance for the conference center does not preclude the same sense of arrival.

ORIENTATION SETTINGS

Arrival represents only the initial step in a subtle process of transition, however. The guest must be tactfully oriented to a different spatial order and temporal pace, while the tempo and demands of the everyday world still linger. WAT&G's extensive reno-vation of the historic Huntington Hotel in Pasadena for Ritz-Carlton serves to illustrate the use of orientation settings. There, the transition experience has been orchestrated to re-establish the hotel's original sense of idyllic isolation and grandeur as a "winter palace."

The traveler becomes a guest upon entering the lobby with its cool marble, period furnishings, and Oriental carpet. Here the guest can look out at a sequence of spaces, through the inner courtyard with its elaborate garden, to the lobby lounge and beyond to the expansive green. The entry experience, like the imagery which preceded it, supports the guest's expectation of a particular period and place. The width of the lobby, with front desk and concierge on either side, the fine appointments, and the view to the inner courtyard compel the guest to surrender the routine of "checking-in" to a pampering host. One immediately senses an order to these spaces and perceives that the ritual of entry and transition will involve a leisurely paced sequence along arcades and galleries.

The main promenade escorts guests from the public arrival to the more private, social spaces that lie just beyond. Past a series of carefully restored rooms, this promenade finally terminates at a vista that draws attention to the restored Horseshoe Garden and trellis-covered Picture Bridge. This sequence of orientation settings gracefully transports the guest to another time and place that might not be accessible in a less skillfully crafted environment.

PUBLIC REALMS & PRIVATE REALMS

Leisure involves both solitude and sociability, and so the resort must offer a mix of public and private realms that can be explored over the length of a visit. In many resorts the guest experience is compromised by a lack of balance between these two complementary requirements. The transition from private to public cannot be addressed through a sequential series of spaces like the entry experience. The guest needs to be able to move easily from one realm to the other.

In the Four Seasons Hotel Mexico City, this balance has been achieved in the heart of the world's most frenetic and populated city. Located along the busy Paseo de la Reforma, the hotel immediately provides a cool oasis as the visitor enters the porte cochere, a grotto-like space sheltered by the structure of the hotel supported on four pier walls. The main entry does not open onto a lobby space, but rather to a long living room with a fireplace wall. Only after entering the semi-private, social realm established by this living room does one turn to the reception lobby.

From there the guest looks out to a vaulted arcade which, in the tradition of Colonial Mexico, signals an interface between another public and private realm. The colonnade circles an interior courtyard and fountain, mediating between a gallery of dining rooms and meeting "salons" which open onto the courtyard. The guest can move easily between these spaces in which "public" and "private" is largely determined by the user.

POINTS OF INTERFACE

The delicate balance between public and private realms brings us to what is perhaps the most intriguing feature of the destination — the search for authenticity. To find the *genus loci*, that which is most genuine about a place, the guest must seek out the "host." The host includes not only the various personnel providing services to the guest, but the indigenous population and their lifeways. Typically this kind of interaction is not easily accessed.

Like the theater, the resort can be characterized as having a front-of-house and back-of-house reality, in which the latter is off-limits to the guest. The kitchens, laundry, offices, equipment areas, and service corridors are kept from view to maintain distance from the everyday world.

On a broader scale there are often similar constraints on interfacing with the local culture. Indeed, in some circumstances the lack of interaction is essential for cultural preservation. However, in the majority of cases, there are mutual benefits to be gained by creating points of interaction between guests and hosts, if the interface does not compromise the integrity of the culture.

The resort at Tanjong Jara and the linked Rantau Abang Visitor Center in Kuala Terengganu, Malaysia serve as an example. The resort is organized to resemble a Malaysian village nestled along a freshwater stream. The resort cottages, which vary in size from one to eight guest rooms, are based upon the architecture of the *istanas* (sultans' palaces). These pavilions required superb local craftsmanship, including intricate woodwork, customized ceramics, locally-made bisque roof tiles, lattice soffits, and steeply pitched roofs with gable grills.

The project created an expanded demand for local crafts which extended to the production of kites, traditional shadow puppets, wood carvings, and woven mats. The result was a legitimate point of interface between hotel guests and their Malaysian hosts, from which the lifeways of a unique culture could be accessed.

The second point of interface involved an equally delicate relationship between the visitors and another indigenous population. The site was part of the migratory route of the giant sea turtles that for centuries have sought out the grassy sand banks formed between the ocean and the Kabang River. The Rantau Abang Visitor Center, which is located five miles from the resort itself, was conceived as a means of protecting the turtles as one of the more precious natural assets of this region. In far too many instances the growth of tourism has diminished the natural attributes of a place, threatening the essential character the traveler seeks in the quest for authenticity. Here, the architecture is at once an observatory for the tourist and a protective rampart for the turtles.

AUTHENTICITY AND FANTASY:
BALANCING DUALITIES

Essential for the transformative experience sought by the tourist is the experience of dualities, whose dynamic tension provokes the tourist to reconsider things, to view the world from a different perspective. The dualities are varied: guests and hosts, solitude and engagement, nature and artifice, access and protection, familiarity and otherness, the real and the imagined. It is this last duality, between authenticity and fantasy, that presents some of the greatest challenges and opportunities in creating the destination.

The project that best conveys this duality is The Palace of The Lost City in South Africa. The challenge was to create an international destination in a place in which the recent history of colonialism, apartheid, and tribal rivalries cast political intonations on traditional architectural forms. Fantasy became the device through which the authentic could be accessed. Here, a fantasy architecture combining elements of 13th-century Islamic mosques, African nativist art, and the exotic palaces of the lost city of Cordoba were combined to create an "archeological discovery" of an ancient civilization. The Palace is a rococo-like invention, which borrows architectural elements from a variety of sources — the Umayyads, the Abbasids, and Byzantium — to convey

an exuberant image of a lost culture. It is entirely a fiction, yet the imagery conveys the possibility of a blending of cultures, the genesis of a great civilization that might have been. The fantasy provides access to speculation and, in a period of uncertainty and transition, inspires a sense of hope.

THE IMAGERY OF A TREASURED PLACE

The visit is transitory. The guest must eventually return to the everyday world of established routines and known places. Yet the destination experience alters the traveler's perspective of his context and possibly his purpose.

If the image of the far-off place offers the hope of fulfillment, the recollected image of the visited place provides the promise of renewal. In this sense the destination remains linked to that alternative destiny, a possible life pursued through speculation,

reflection, engagement, and experience. The traveler approaches this objective as before, through the agency of the journey, the medium of the dream, and the presence of the destination place. And yet, there is a difference, for once the destination has been experienced, the dream is informed by the memory of a previous moment and the journey is motivated by a return to a cherished place.

The image of the destination becomes that of a treasured place, a trove of experiences and stored reflections, that provides the traveler with the resources necessary to navigate a routinized life and to pursue a purposeful one. The architects of the destination, like the travelers they hope to accommodate, are in pursuit of an ideal place, approached through journeys of imagination and guided by dreams of transformation.

HOSPITALITY PROJECTS

HOTEL BORA BORA

Bora Bora, for all of its worldwide name recognition, is only a tiny island (four miles long and two and a half miles wide) with just one main road and one stop sign. The fact that this French Polynesian paradise is not easy to get to (it lies 120 miles northwest of the island of Tahiti) only enhances its appeal to certain travelers.

Designed to be unobtrusive, the resort doesn't outshout its surroundings; it feels like a genuine Tahitian village with a South Seas atmosphere. The setting provides unobstructed views of the lagoon and Mount Otemanu, while offering splendid isolation; bungalows and villas are hidden from the road by lush gardens and fruit trees.

In keeping with the use of indigenous materials and styles, the 80 native-style *fares* (bungalows) are constructed of cedar, and each has bamboo walls and roofs made with hand-tied pandanus thatch. Fifteen of these are suspended on stilts over the water. All of the open-air buildings take advantage of the natural cooling of the trade winds.

Incorporating regional influences, the design of the Hotel Bora Bora affords great economy, in both construction and operations. Use of readily available materials capitalizes on local resources, and eliminates the need for air conditioning and other expensive, high-maintenance building elements.

The merging of modern comforts with Tahitian authenticity is apparent in the resort's high level of personal service and in the guest accommodations.

The rooms are large (some, nearly 800 square feet) and most include a separate living room, a four-poster bed, and a private deck which leads directly to the water.

The Hotel Bora Bora is the epitome of tranquility and, at the same time, rich in its recreational offerings; visitors can choose to participate in water-oriented activities like scuba diving, snorkeling, fishing excursions, catamaran sails, sunset cruises, and waterskiing. Helicopter flights and a jeep safari tour are also available to adventurous guests. Local produce and seafood are featured in the hotel's restaurant, which fits the simultaneous descriptions of fine and informal dining.

LOCATION
Bora Bora
French Polynesia

CLIENT
Société Hôtelière de Tahara'a
J.M. Long & Co., Inc.

SITE SIZE
16 acres

PROJECT SIZE
80 bungalows

AMENITIES
Water recreation facilities;
views of lagoon and beach
from every room; tennis courts

The Tahitian-inspired architecture of Hotel Bora Bora adroitly captures the sense of place that gives Bora Bora Island its reputation as one of the most beguilingly beautiful sites in the Pacific.

In the tradition of Tahitian vernacular architecture, fares — thatched-roof bungalows — form a village-like grouping of informal, open-air structures.

Guest bungalows — some perched on stilts directly over the lagoon — feature high ceilings of hand-tied pandanus thatch, wood siding, private, lanai-decks with deep shade, and large rooms opening onto expansive views.

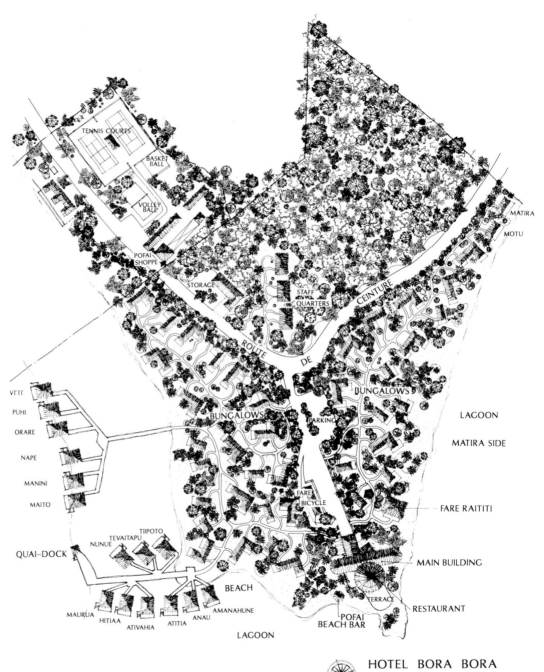

TENNIS COURTS

BASKET BALL

VOLLEY BALL

POFAI SHOPPE

STORAGE

STAFF QUARTERS

ROUTE DE CEINTURE

MATIRA MOTU

BUNGALOWS

BUNGALOWS

PARKING

LAGOON

MATIRA SIDE

VETE

PUHI

ORARE

NAPE

MANINI

MAITO

FARE BICYCLE

FARE RAITITI

QUAI-DOCK

TIIPOTO

TEVAITAPU

NUNUE

MAIN BUILDING

BEACH

TERRACE

RESTAURANT

MAURUA

HITIAA

ATIVAHIA

ATITIA

ANAU

AMANAHUNE

POFAI BEACH BAR

LAGOON

HOTEL BORA BORA

METERS 1:500
0 10 20 40

RAMADA GREAT BARRIER REEF RESORT

As INTERNATIONAL RESORT development consumes more and more of this planet's unspoiled beach frontage, concern for the natural environment grows. It is no wonder that local Cairns residents were worried about a resort hotel planned for a site with a beachside grove of palms and 800-year-old melaluca (paper bark) trees.

However, in the case of the Ramada Great Barrier Reef Resort, both developer and architect were determined to preserve the integrity of the site as well as the ancient trees. Working from aerial photographs, WAT&G developed a tree-sparing plan so that the trees, not the buildings, would dominate.

All the major trees were retained; the building was designed to be a part of the forest rather than apart from it. (Such was the commitment, there was even a penalty clause imposed on the builder for damage to any of the trees.) The three- and four-story hotel now nestles among the palm and melaluca trees and wraps around a central courtyard featuring a large, free-form swimming pool. Both the pool and the building weave and notch to leave the

trees undisturbed.

Ninety light-brown, poured-concrete columns that support the building were cast in a mold made from an indigenous log, giving each column a remarkable tree-like appearance. Balcony planters obscure indoor/outdoor boundaries and also contribute to a sense of being among the trees.

The pool shape generally follows the contours of an existing swamp and is constructed above ground to avoid damaging the tree roots. Timber decking at the pool's edge forms tree "wells" which leave undisturbed islands of vegetation in their natural habitat.

Not only did the main site dictate where to locate the resort amenities (such as spa, pre-conference deck, and outdoor coffee plaza), "left-over" areas did the same: a sunken children's playground incorporates a large, shade-providing tree; a leafy tropical nook became a hammock area; and a secluded hideaway beckons with a fruit garden area.

The creation of the Ramada Great Barrier Reef Resort has demonstrated unequivocally that development and conservation can occur harmoniously. Its success proves that environmentally responsive design can be good for business, as well.

LOCATION
*Palm Cove
Cairns, Australia*

CLIENT
*International Resort
Pty. Australia*

SITE SIZE
5 acres

PROJECT SIZE
*150,000 square feet,
200 rooms*

AMENITIES
*Central courtyard;
free-form swimming pool;
private balconies;
children's play area;
conference facilities*

Footbridges criss-cross the elevated pool, which flows under the three-story building in places. The building code, in response to flood potential, prohibits ground-floor guest rooms.

The palm-studded, light-filled lobby establishes the easy informality of this small, environmentally sensitive resort. The Ramada Great Barrier Reef Resort is designed to live comfortably with the heat, moisture, and periodic flooding typical of Far North Queensland.

The above-ground pool — built around existing trees — is suspended to eliminate damage to tree roots.

FOUR SEASONS HOTEL MEXICO CITY

LOCATION
Mexico City, Mexico

CLIENT
Proparmex S.A. de C.V.

SITE SIZE
1.75 acres

PROJECT SIZE
*347,000 square feet,
8 stories, 240 guest rooms*

AMENITIES
*Indoor-outdoor restaurant;
cafe; private business center;
health club; rooftop pool area;
12,000 square feet of
meeting, banquet and
conference facilities equipped
with state-of-the-art
audio/visual services*

THE SITE IS IN THE MIDST of the world's largest city, on the *Paseo de la Reforma,* one of the world's busiest and loveliest boulevards. Nearby is the famed *Zona Rosa,* Mexico's premier shopping area. In this bustling location, the client wished to provide an intimate, refined, European-style hotel which would attract high-level corporate executives and professionals traveling to Mexico City on business. The hotel was also planned as an elegant social setting for affluent local residents.

The design philosophy was to create a secluded retreat in the center of this enormous, vibrant city. The design does not attempt to mirror its immediate urban surroundings. Rather, it respects the traditions of European-inspired Mexican architecture and is derived from a blending of Spanish Colonial and historic French influences. Mexico's heritage of Spanish Colonial architecture is reflected in the exterior facade with its understated detail and use of simple materials — stone, wood, stucco, and tile — and in the inward, sequestered focus of the hotel — its central courtyard and the colonnade which surrounds it.

The French historic tradition of Mexico City was integrated into the design to refine spaces and to add detailing, light, and atmosphere. It is evident in the use of wrought iron, such as handrails along the second floor colonnade and courtyard benches and in the finished woods, marble, stained glass, glazed doors, and mullioned windows that lend character and definition to the overall design.

One element which contributes to the private feeling of the hotel is a low, coffered, formal carriage entrance. The guest who arrives by car leaves the congestion of major thoroughfares behind and encounters this dimly lit space. The entry, with its stone paving, glass lanterns, and mullioned doors, opens into the lobby, which in turn opens into the serenity of the courtyard. The effect is soothing, charming.

The large central courtyard provides an oasis of quiet and becomes the focal point for dining and for meetings held in the hotel. It provides natural light, with the lushness of vegetation and the sounds and sights of a fountain. It also ensures enjoyable views for most of the guest rooms.

The courtyard of the Four Seasons Hotel Mexico City is the heart and soul of the design and of the hotel itself.

The design of the hotel, with its emphasis on a decorative central fountain and colonnade surrounding an inner courtyard, borrows from Mexico's long heritage of Spanish Colonial architecture.

24

Mexico City's historic French influence emerges here in the wrought iron scrollwork of banisters, in French decorative elements, and in the sweeping turn of a staircase below high, arched windows.

The design philosophy — as exemplified in the health club and pool area — was to create an elegant and serene environment in the midst of an enormous, vibrant city.

THE CLIENT WANTED nothing less than a palace by the sea. There was to be a romance to the work which would blend with Florida's history, sunlight, landscape, and the particular, extraordinary site. The 463-room Ritz-Carlton, Naples, located directly on a three-mile stretch of white sand beach on Florida's southwest coast and part of the master-planned Pelican Bay

THE RITZ-CARLTON, NAPLES

community, is thus a hotel in the grand style of an earlier era.

One influence was The Breakers, Henry Flagler's famed resort hotel in Palm Beach, which was fashioned after the alluring villas of Italy. Like its forebear, The Ritz-Carlton, Naples has twin belvedere towers, gracefully arched windows, an arcade with classic balustrades of molded stone, and expansive French doors for each guest room. The 14-story tower gives stateliness to the scale of the hotel and is in character with the rest of the development, which includes high-rise structures. Building skyward also leaves room on the relatively narrow 19-acre site for terrace landscaping, English rose gar-

dens, seven tennis courts, a breezy veranda, a swimming pool, and a casual beachside restaurant. The resort is planned to take full advantage of a prime beachfront location; the building's U-shape, with guest wings perpendicular to the strand, gives every guest room an ocean view.

The proportions of the interior are as timeless and lavishly scaled as those of the exterior. Off the two-level lobby, a grand staircase climbs to the mezzanine and its 23,280 square feet of ballrooms and meeting spaces.

Site requirements were strict. All habitable spaces had to be at least 13 feet above the natural grade for flood control. A delicate ecosystem of untouched, jungle-like wetlands that now separates formal gardens from the beach was carefully protected. At two beach-access points, boardwalks bridge the mass of wetland shrubs and mangroves.

The Ritz-Carlton, Naples reflects the classical architecture of the turn-of-the-century gilded hotels that made Florida a visitor's mecca. While amply fulfilling all the requirements of a modern-day five-star resort, in style, detailing, colors, and materials, it is a stately reminder of another age.

The lobby stands above grade for flood protection and to allow ocean views over a protected mangrove swamp. A molded-stone arcade flanks the rear of the hotel, overlooking terraced gardens that echo the axial symmetry of the tower's design.

The grand scale exterior of the Ritz-Carlton, Naples features twin belvedere towers and is reminiscent of the monumental villas of Italy and the turn-of-the-century hotels of Florida, which reflected their Italian legacy.

Rich materials and
lavish proportions in the
public areas of the hotel
replay the architectural
theme of a timeless,
classically scaled design.

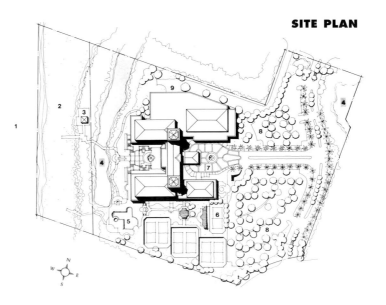

1. Gulf of Mexico
2. Beach
3. Beach Gazebo
4. Lagoon
5. Pool
6. Center Court
7. Motor Court
8. Parking
9. Service Entrance

HYATT REGENCY KAUAI

LOCATION
*Poipu Beach, Kauai, Hawaii
USA*

CLIENT
*Ainako Development Corporation
and Kawailoa Development*

SITE SIZE
50 oceanfront acres

PROJECT SIZE
*759,300 square feet,
600 guest rooms*

AMENITIES
*5 restaurants; 5 lounges;
65,000 square feet of banquet
and meeting facilities;
12,000 square feet of retail space;
25,000-square-foot health
and fitness spa; multiple water
features; 4 tennis courts;
18-hole Robert Trent Jones II
championship golf course*

CLEARLY, HYATT REGENCY KAUAI is a world apart from Hawaiian grass shack architecture; yet *purely, elegantly Hawaiian, the feel of old Hawaii,* and an *enticing image of old Hawaii* are guest comments heard repeatedly.

How is it that a 600-room hotel with 759,300 square feet of floor space in a series of two- and four-story stucco-clad masonry buildings with massive, glazed terra cotta tile roofs and a lot of marble elicits, "Now, *this* is what a Hawaiian hotel should be — ". The answer: site sensitivity and the appeal of a Hawaii-evolved architecture that *feels* right for the instinctively informal tropical island mind-set, even when that architecture is monumental in scope, elegant in detail.

Nature's spectacular setting for Hyatt Regency Kauai is its legacy and its challenge. Under a brilliant unpolluted sky in a rural neighborhood, sited on 50 oceanfront acres warmed year-round by temperate sun, cooled by prevailing trade winds, and framed by verdant mountains (nearby Mount Waialeale is called the wettest spot on earth), the hotel emerges as a central pavilion with buildings that radiate from its core through inviting waterways and lavish gardens.

The designer and developer worked closely to take advantage of nature's scenic gifts, while minimizing her wilder aspects. A series of man-made lagoons, pools, and other water features establishes and dramatizes the lush, tropical settings — and lures guests away from an unsafe surf. Building materials — from stainless-steel hardware, and epoxy-coated rebars to air filters for outside air intakes — were selected to weather the corrosiveness of the salt-laden air.

In consideration of brisk winds, buildings were grouped formally to establish courtyards in the wind's lee. In consideration of potential hurricane-force winds, the main buildings were sited upslope and well behind the legal setback from the ocean. The value of this precaution was made clear in 1992, when Hyatt Kauai took the full force of Hurricane Iniki's 160-mile-per-hour winds and came through the ordeal with full structural integrity.

Eschewing a glitzy, action-packed, carnival-like concept for the hotel, the Island-born developer, together with his Island-born architect, decided to have Hyatt Regency Kauai speak quietly, with confidence, as a seductively romantic echo of Hawaii of the 1920s and 1930s in a style now widely labeled Hawaiian classic.

A *striking example of Hawaiian classic architecture, the Hyatt Regency Kauai embraces the outdoors but works largely within a vocabulary of formal elements and monumental size. Curvilinear protrusions extending into a salt-water lagoon further dramatize the Seaview Terrace, which is already made spectacular by the great height of its columns and a splendid view of the Pacific Ocean.*

Landscaping was designed to be a common thread for the whole hotel project, unifying all elements in a complementary relationship. A meandering river pool is part of a variety of water elements throughout the landscape.

Not nearly as fragile as it looks, the thatched roof Tidepools restaurant was gutted during Hurricane Iniki but remained structurally sound thanks to an under-roof of concrete, concrete piles, and a concrete foundation. A nod to the spirit of early Hawaiian architecture, Tidepools stands in contrast to its overpowering contemporary "cousin." Although the two buildings differ vastly, their common openness acknowledges the characterizing uniqueness of Hawaii's climate and architecture.

33

A *bronze, thrownet fisherman is poised on the rocks outside the thatched-roof restaurant, a larger-than-life example of the resort's focus on Hawaiian culture.*

T *he 600-room resort stretches out among lush gardens and lagoons in a series of attached four-story buildings radiating from a central pavilion. Massive, double-pitched roofs of ceramic tile mirror the garden-green hues of the countryside.*

At the Hyatt Regency Kauai, "out" may be "in" and "in" is almost always nearly outside. Many walls open to wide courts, gardens, and beautiful views. Symmetry contributes to the building's quiet stateliness, while the flow of open spaces keeps the atmosphere informal.

The play of woodwork against white stucco adds interest to the lobby's Seaview Lounge. The vaulted ceiling, with exposed beams, window and door detailing, and koa wood cabinetry, suggests Plantation-era architecture.

Stevenson's Library (so named for Robert Louis Stevenson, who spent time in Hawaii in the late nineteenth century) "wraps" guests in the treasured patina of Acacia koa wall paneling. Unique to Hawaii, this hardwood is prized for its beauty, strength, and workability.

For most of the twentieth century Kauai's economy has been intertwined with the cultivation of sugar cane. Graceful cane leaves are a design motif in the Ilima Terrace restaurant, where stylized metal greenery forms a grill around the top of the high-ceilinged room.

SHANGRI-LA HOTEL, GARDEN WING

THE GARDEN WING ADDITION to the Shangri-La Hotel was designed to provide the existing high-rise urban hotel with additional guest rooms that were larger and more luxurious than those in the original wing. Rather than design an annex to the existing building, the architects conceived the Garden Wing as a separate and distinct sculpture with a low profile to balance the tall, narrow form of its neighbor. Architecturally, the Garden Wing draws its inspiration from the structural motif of the original building, which features a barrel vault roof. Incorporating the curves of the original roof system, the architects chose to flop them horizontally for use as the Garden Wing's structural theme. The distinguishing scalloped shape of the plan gives the building a strong identity. The facade of the building — which includes rounded balconies for every guest room — steps backwards as its height increases, forming a basic "A" frame.

The exterior is only a prelude to the spectacular nine-story atrium garden inside (the first ever to be built in Singapore). With the goal of fusing the indoors and outdoors, the designers brought greenery into the heart of the building. Over 45,000 plants — including 110 varieties of palms, trees, ferns, vines, and rows of red bougainvillea — contribute to this lush garden environment. So extensive was the hotel's landscaping that a project nursery was established on-site. The vast tropical atrium lobby focuses on a waterfall cascading from its source two stories above ground into a rock-bordered pool below.

Corridors, open to the atrium, are connected on the upper floors by bridges which serve as struts for the structural framework. Walking across these bridges, guests get a breathtaking view of the sky above and the gardens below.

Landscape elements — foliage, waterfalls, bridges, and paths — provide the resort complex with a unifying force both inside and out. The garden motif further reinforces Singapore's identity in Asia as the Garden City.

LOCATION
Orange Grove Road
Singapore

CLIENT
Shangri-La Hotel

SITE SIZE
12 acres

PROJECT SIZE
165 guest rooms

AMENITIES
Open atrium lobby
with waterfalls; sauna rooms;
squash and tennis courts

An addition to an existing high-rise, the nine-story Garden Wing presents a strong sculptural character. Bower-like balconies echo the vertical curvilinear concept in the rooftop vaults of the original structure.

A striking example of "landscape as architecture," the Shangri-La Garden Wing reinforces Singapore's identity as Asia's Garden City. Single-loaded corridors face an open-air atrium, which provide a base for nine floors of hanging gardens. Atrium waterfalls mute urban noise, enhancing the garden experience.

HYATT REGENCY CHEJU

LOCATION
Cheju Island, Korea

CLIENT
Namju Development Co.

SITE SIZE
10 acres

PROJECT SIZE
224 rooms

AMENITIES
*Eight-story atrium;
tennis courts;
indoor/outdoor swimming pool;
nightclub; casino*

OFF THE SOUTHERNMOST PENINSULA of South Korea is Cheju Island, called the "Emerald Isle of Asia" for the lushness of its forests, mountains, and beaches. It is on this pristine oasis that WAT&G was asked to design the island's first international resort hotel, thereby setting the standard for eight subsequent hotel/entertainment complexes that were part of a master plan for the region. Designing the flagship hotel in a destination resort is a significant responsibility in view of its influence on the success of future development and value of the surrounding property for years to come.

Added to that design challenge was the logistical task of coordinating an international team: the owners were in Seoul; the hotel operators in Chicago; the interior designers in Hong Kong; many of the manufacturers were in Japan; the associate architects were in Korea; and the design architects were in Hawaii.

The result: a world-class resort hotel that appeals to both Korean and Western tastes. Two domed structures sit on a dramatic promontory overlooking the island, one of which features an eight-story-high central atrium, the other, a casino. Their design is reminiscent of the indigenous Cheju homes with a stone base and a domed thatch roof. The cultural form of the octagon, derived from traditional Korean art forms, creates the inherent geometry for the structure.

The challenge to design a resort hotel that appeals to two essentially different guest profiles is illustrated by the accommodations themselves: 40 of the hotel's 224 rooms feature *ondol* floors, which allow guests to sleep on futons and enjoy the radiant heat coming from coils underneath the finished flooring. The deck of the indoor pool and the floors of private dining rooms in the Korean-style restaurant also incorporate *ondol* flooring.

To attract the international traveler, the resort features a casino, which is connected to the hotel's lobby by an arcade in which visitors can choose from a range of shopping and eating options. The popularity of the hotel exceeded the expectations of the owners. WAT&G was asked to design a significant expansion to include: 70 guest rooms and 30 suites; a new health club and spa; a multi-entertainment center with water slides; as well as additional space in the casino, the restaurants, the function area, and the shopping arcade.

Ubiquitous and revered on Cheju, the stone grandfather, Tolharubang, represents fertility.

The atrium — the first ever in Korea — captures the atmosphere of the outdoors, complete with rockscapes, palm trees, and lush vegetation. Two waterfalls flow from a lagoon: one spilling into the heated indoor pool, the other cascading past two restaurants and into the outdoor pool.

The hotel mounts a dramatic promontory, offering a 360-degree vista of Cheju Island. The building includes an eight-story octagonal main structure, a separate and smaller octagonal casino structure, and a retail arcade joining the two buildings.

Each of the hotel's 224 rooms has its own private terrace with a sea or garden view. The domed buildings recall the island's indigenous architectural form: a thatched-roof, octagonal, stone folk-hut.

THE RITZ-CARLTON, RANCHO MIRAGE

FOR MORE THAN FIFTY YEARS, the low-desert climate of Southern California's Coachella Valley has lured Hollywood luminaries, year-round residents, and vacationers. On a 24-acre hillside bluff overlooking the community of Rancho Mirage, the client planned to build a luxurious and exclusive destination resort.

The architectural design was influenced by two primary considerations — climate and setting. The weather in this area is the driest and warmest in all of California — with 350 days of sunshine a year. The design follows climate in welcoming guests to enjoy the outdoors; airy courtyards are abundant, and each guest room has a balcony. Ample terraces extend from lobby lounge, restaurants, and conference facilities toward the pool, adjacent lawns, and outdoor dining areas.

In the clear dry air of the desert, sun control is a major consideration. The design for The Ritz-Carlton, Rancho Mirage employs long roof overhangs and deep balconies to shield both guests and structures. Pale colors also temper the desert climate by reflecting light and heat.

A major concern throughout the planning stages of the design was to retain the natural characteristics of the site. Thus, the hotel is relatively small — 240 rooms. Because the resort is situated near the Santa Rosa Mountain refuge of the endangered desert bighorn sheep, a low-impact design that makes use of subtle color and stonework was developed.

Natural materials are used in the facades and retaining walls. A Wright-influenced design concept is evident in the continuous horizontal lines and the emphatically low roof-pitch of the buildings, which give center stage to the surrounding terrain of weathered boulders and desert ringed by mountains. The design was planned to be refined and non-imposing in an environment that is spectacular in its own right; even the landfill is colored to blend with the indigenous soil.

High above the valley known in ancient times as the hollow of God's hand and in modern times as the greatest desert resort community in the world, The Ritz-Carlton, Rancho Mirage stands as an elegant and serene oasis.

LOCATION
*Rancho Mirage, California
USA*

CLIENT
Partnership of Federated Development Co./The Ritz-Carlton Hotel Company

SITE SIZE
24 acres

PROJECT SIZE
*208,000 square feet,
240 guest rooms*

AMENITIES
*Pool and fitness center;
8,400-square-foot ballroom;
ten-court tennis facility*

Twelve years of planning assured that the native desert bighorn sheep are protected in their natural habitat. A bronze sculpture of the sheep welcomes guests at the entrance to the resort.

In a desert ringed with mountains, The Ritz-Carlton, Rancho Mirage appears to be carved from the bluff. Angled eaves and eave fascias echo the mountainous background, and low, unimposing lines are appropriate to the site.

A *dramatic entry with palms and stone walls leads to this paradoxical desert enclave, an oasis in the wilderness. Stone, neutral plaster, shallow roofs, and strong horizontal lines blend with a rugged landscape.*

A*cross from the entry road to the hotel lies the tennis clubhouse, designed to complement the architecture of the main building.*

SITE PLAN

1. Porte Cochere
2. Lobby
3. Ballroom
4. Guest Room Wing
5. Pool
6. Cafe & Terrace
7. Access to
   Underground Parking
8. Service Yard

Operating with directives from the Coastal Zone Management Commission of the Virgin Islands, the design team set out to preserve a significant ecological site, while boosting the local economy through the creation of a five-star resort.

The 15-acre, bowl-shaped site surrounds a large salt pond, which attracts migratory and native birds, marine life, deer, iguana,

GRAND PALAZZO RESORT

and mongeese. The pond acts as an important sediment basin, absorbing most of the drainage from the immediate area and extending the coastline through the stabilizing roots of its mangrove trees.

Initially, the design team evaluated the complex's potential interaction with wildlife in the salt pond. The team's main concern was to preserve the environment so that terrestrial and marine life could continue to reproduce.

As a result of the team's study, the design preserves the salt pond in its entirety as a major feature in the resort. Natural stone walls surround the lagoon to prevent erosion and to protect breeding ducks and

other wildlife. A seawall along the beach provides further erosion control for the entire basin. Greenery in this area is kept primarily native, with imports selected to support the local and migratory fauna.

Throughout the site are abundant walking paths and open spaces; bulldozing was kept to a minimum. Automobile traffic is excluded from the grounds, and parking is hidden.

The architectural design plan divides the resort into relatively small-scale components with low, unobtrusive lines. Six three-story guest buildings and a separate dining facility are placed in a semicircle that borders the pond and overlooks the bay.

Doors open along the entire length of the dining pavilion to provide natural cooling. For additional energy conservation and economy, the resort has its own generator and desalination plant. All waste water is recycled and is used to irrigate various areas of landscape. The heat process used to desalinate the water turns out steam, which powers a generator for the on-site laundry.

The Grand Palazzo succeeds both as a world-class resort and as an attractive design that preserves its fragile, coastal environment.

LOCATION
St. Thomas
U.S. Virgin Islands

CLIENT
Pemberton Resorts

SITE SIZE
15 acres

PROJECT SIZE
218,808 square feet,
150 guest rooms

AMENITIES
2 restaurants; swimming pool;
4 tennis courts;
water-sports facility;
meeting rooms;
fitness center; beach bar

Six guest buildings and the dining pavilion form a wide crescent around a carefully preserved salt pond; the pond becomes a major design element of the project, and a cloistered effect is achieved on the 15-acre, bowl-shaped site.

The oceanfront setting is the most important element of the design. Low density, spacious grounds, retaining walls made up of stone taken from the property, and secluded parking direct attention to the nearby beach and island views.

A primary consideration was to merge the guest buildings with the site. All courtyards in the accommodation blocks are finished in a fossil-like courtyard stone that blends with the native landscape.

Materials used in the classical Mediterranean-style buildings are designed to withstand hurricanes. All structures are of concrete masonry with operable windows for natural cooling.

THE RITZ-CARLTON, KAPALUA

In the process of planning this resort, an ancient Hawaiian burial ground was discovered in the beachfront area where the hotel building was to be placed. This turned out to be a massive archeological site containing nearly 1000 graves, and the project was halted. After a two-year delay, the architects relocated the building up a hill and redesigned it to fit into the hillside, thereby preserving the sizeable burial ground.

One of the largest Ritz-Carlton resort properties, the Kapalua project was designed to give guests the feeling of intimacy inherent in a much smaller structure. To reduce the visual impact, 550 guest rooms were spread among six buildings, each six stories in height and stepped down a slope towards the coast.

For the same reason, public areas in the hotel were divided into three separate buildings, including a center main lobby building that opens out to an expansive view of the ocean, the 11,000-square-foot pool, and the richly landscaped hotel grounds. To the extent possible, service spaces were placed below grade into the hillside and away from guests' sight.

Each building was angled independently to maximize the guests' views of the north Maui coastline and the famous Kapalua Bay golf course.

The resort's architectural and interior design tries to balance the high-end style of a Ritz with the more casual requirements of an island resort. This was accomplished by designing for fluidity between inside and outside. Architects were challenged to create an open-air feeling suited to the unpredictable climate of Kapalua, which can be quite windy. Large sliding glass panels draw the visitor across the elegant public spaces to a commanding exterior view of the Hawaiian sea and sky.

Designed to respect the existing architectural style of Kapalua and Pineapple Hill plantation areas, the simple building forms have distinguishable grey-blue roofs with deep overhangs. The pineapple theme — a symbol of both Hawaiian hospitality and the working pineapple plantation on Maui — is used as a decorative element on balcony railings. Cast into concrete panels are Hawaiian floral patterns which further reflect the hotel's location.

In spite of the feeling of intimacy created by diminishing the mass of the building, the hotel actually encompasses 30,000 square feet of indoor meeting space, including a 16,000-square-foot ballroom; a 165-seat amphitheater; and ten permanent meeting rooms — some with fireplaces, all with majestic views. So important is this property's site to local residents and to visitors seeking a Hawaiian experience, the hotel has established an in-house Hawaii Committee to help ensure the ongoing support and preservation of Hawaiiana.

LOCATION
Kapalua, Maui, Hawaii
USA

CLIENT
Kaptel Associates

SITE SIZE
38.5 acres

PROJECT SIZE
550 guest rooms
(including 58 suites)

AMENITIES
Three-tiered swimming pool with cascading waterfalls; 10 oceanfront tennis courts; conference facilities including a ballroom for 1,400, surrounded by three championship golf courses

The Ritz-Carlton, Kapalua was designed with attention to the small decorative details that reflect its Hawaiian setting.

The resort's nine separate buildings, each angled to maximize views, step down towards the coast.

50

Through large sliding glass panels, the view of Hawaiian sea and sky looks like a painting from inside the reception lobby.

The balance of elegance and informality is evidenced in the hotel's suites.

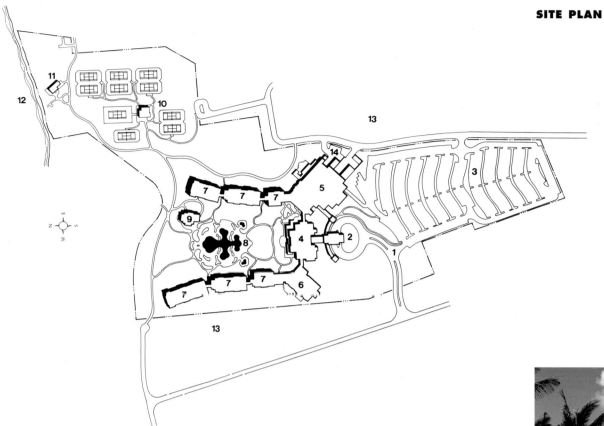

SITE PLAN

1. Main Entry
2. Porte Cochere
3. Guest Parking
4. Center Lobby Building
5. East Ballroom/Meeting room
6. West Restaurant/Fitness Building
7. Guest Room Building
8. Pool
9. Pool Bar/Restaurant
10. Tennis Center
11. Beach Facility/Bar
12. Pacific Ocean
13. Golf Course
14. Service Yard

A *trellised canopy provides shade for informal outdoor dining and frames the view towards the swimming pool and ocean beyond.*

A *three-tiered, 11,000-square-foot swimming pool includes cascading waterfalls.*

GOA, THE FORMER PORTUGUESE colony on India's western coastline, is known for its beautiful beaches and temperate climate. Called *A Perola do Orienta* by the Portuguese conquistador who discovered it, Goa is still the Pearl of the Orient to those who visit.

As they approach this resort, which is set on the coast of the Arabian Sea, visitors get

GOA RENAISSANCE RESORT

a glimpse of a vaulted dome with four grand gothic arches sitting like a crown atop the hotel's atrium. Visiting primarily from Germany, England, France, Italy, and other parts of India, guests enter through a portico whose colonnade porch leads them to the lobby through an open arch.

The feeling of grandeur is not left at the entrance. Sounds of waterfalls, and patterns of light pouring in from colored glass in the arched skylights, lend drama to the two-story atrium.

The resort is expansive in its feel but not at a cost to the site itself. No buildings in the complex are higher than any of the 200 trees on the property. So important were

environmental concerns to the client, that they played an important part in shaping the resort's development. Setbacks exceeded local laws; a sewage treatment plant was built to recycle gray water; and a 7.4-mile pipeline was installed to bring fresh water from a reservoir into the complex.

Along with the land, the culture itself became a source for design inspiration. The flying buttress — a familiar design element in local churches of Goa — can be found throughout the hotel's public spaces. Pointed arches and columns are also borrowed from Goan architecture. The beams that support the atrium roof were laid out as they would be in traditional Goan homes. The local influence can also be found in the interiors, which feature ceramic mosaic flooring, intricate wood and stone carvings, and design motifs of birds and flowers.

Most of the 190 guest rooms are oriented toward the sea and around a swimming complex. Two wings lead out from either flank of the lobby/central atrium and step down toward the sea in three tiers. Indeed, this Pearl of the Orient shines brightly for those who experience Goa.

LOCATION
Salcette, Goa
India

CLIENT
Sunder G. Advani
Ramada Hotels India

SITE SIZE
23 acres

PROJECT SIZE
190 guest rooms

AMENITIES
Conference center;
two-story atrium;
shopping arcade;
discotheque; lighted tennis courts;
six-hole golf course; jogging track;
7,000 tropical plants

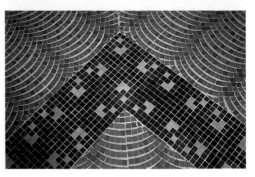

A *free-form pool establishes the recreational focal point of a court formed by guest bungalows and a lobby building. A vaulted dome, with four gothic arches, rises 40 feet above the lobby atrium to crown the resort and proclaim its defining motif.*

FOUR SEASONS RESORT WAILEA

THE CLIENT MADE IT ABUNDANTLY clear: he wanted a palace for his serene 15-acre oceanfront site at Wailea on the Hawaiian island of Maui. He did not have in mind the indigenous grass house with thatched roof that served as palace for Hawaiian chiefs in the centuries before Westerners arrived. His mandate required a 375-room resort hotel of unmistakably regal character. Unstated was the architect's commitment to environmentally appropriate — in this case tropical — architecture.

The concept of "palace" was played out, in part, through the symmetry and formal pattern of the building, its grand stair, courts, gardens, pools, and fountains. A colonnade around the building gives a classic aura and complements a wide-eaved clay-tile roof that is consistent with formality while serving as a much-needed shade device.

Although of palatial style and proportion, with decidedly fine details and furnishings, the resort was designed to be in full harmony with its tropical setting and climate. Throughout the design process the architect used typically tropical devices — cross ventilation; sun-protected and breeze-cooled open spaces; natural lighting; the blurring of boundaries between indoors and outdoors; focus on water for sight, sound, and feel; and the use of lush, exotic plant materials.

In addition to taking full advantage of views, the architect took maximum advantage of warm, year-round temperatures by opening up many of the public spaces. Numerous areas that would ordinarily be perceived as rooms are actually more like deep verandas flowing casually and openly from one to another. Both the fine-dining restaurant and the casual grill offer guests the option of indoor or outdoor dining by day or evening. Hallways in guest room wings, atypically, have natural light and ventilation but no air-conditioning. Conference and banquet rooms — also atypically — have natural light and ocean and/or garden views. Many outdoor spaces were designed to be comfortably shaded from Maui's almost constant sun and cooled by prevailing winds.

It is noteworthy that this kind of design is possible in only a few places in the world and that even when it is combined with a predominantly grand and formal base it can function without compromise, in context with its tropical nature.

LOCATION
Wailea, Maui
Hawaii
USA

CLIENT
Wailea Beach Palace Company
(TSA Development Co. Ltd.)

SITE SIZE
15 oceanfront acres

PROJECT SIZE
558,093 square feet,
375 rooms and suites

AMENITIES
Retail shops; 20,000 square feet
of meeting and function space;
library; children's playroom;
health club; numerous
water features; formal garden;
sculpture garden; luau garden;
2 tennis courts

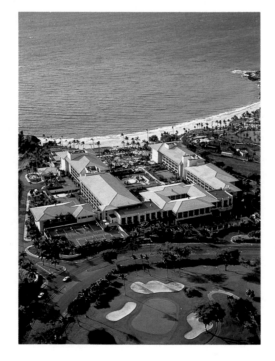

The U-shape of the building, a central courtyard facing the water, and guest rooms placed at a 45-degree angle to corridors give 85 percent of the Four Seasons' guest rooms an ocean view. Colonnades support deep eaves and give shelter to open-air, oceanfront public spaces.

The architectural challenges in the development of this resort were threefold: The client requested 300-400 palatial guest rooms, all entry and public areas near the ocean, and ocean views from most rooms.

The coffered ceilings and columned passages of the richly appointed lobby follow the building's formal approach but also open to the ocean and flow informally from area to area. A variety of finishing methods creates patterns on the limestone flooring.

A *study in grandeur — both natural and manmade — the central courtyard develops the "palace" concept largely through symmetry and cascading fountains. Canopied gazebos and a poolside bar provide shade from year-round tropical sun and give the beachfront complex a casual atmosphere.*

THE RITZ-CARLTON HUNTINGTON HOTEL

LOCATION
*Pasadena, California
USA*

CLIENT
Huntington Hotel Partners

SITE SIZE
23 acres

PROJECT SIZE
*375,000 square feet,
385 guest rooms*

AMENITIES
*Olympic-size pool; 3 tennis courts;
lobby lounge; pool bar/grill;
fitness center; 25,000 square feet
of meeting facilities,
including 12,000-square-foot
grand ballroom, 4,500-square-foot
Viennese Junior Ballroom and
8,500 square feet of additional
meeting and boardrooms*

WHEN THE 87-YEAR-OLD Huntington Hotel was closed in 1985 because it was determined to be unsafe in the event of an earthquake, enormous community concern arose regarding its fate. The Huntington, a part of growing up in Pasadena, had always captivated the local community who shared its particular history of Easter pageants and high school proms, of debutante balls and celebrity fetes.

In 1989, the hotel's new owners commissioned WAT&G to lead a design team in renovating the hotel, through a mixture of approaches: new construction, replication, recreation, recycling, and restoration. The variety of the hotel's components, its large scale, and its historical significance contributed to the complexity of the project. The City of Pasadena stipulated over thirty conditions as a mandate to the design team to preserve the hotel's heritage.

All changes and conversions were carefully considered with the past in mind. Once razed, the central tower was replicated in an exacting manner, to withstand future earthquakes and create modern-day hotel guest rooms. Elements of the original tower, such as fenestration and arched tops of doors, were used in the new design. Roof overhangs were replicated from the original wood construction using contemporary fireproof materials.

Many of the building's spaces were reconfigured for more functional use. The Georgian Room, once a ballroom, became an elegant dining room. The Viennese Room became a junior ballroom. The old kitchen was converted to meeting rooms and retail space. A new 12,000-square-foot ballroom was added to the former service yard.

The original entrance was transformed into the new entry and lobby; it recalls the archway entered in the early 1900s by horse and carriage. The carriage house itself was redesigned as retail and office space.

Several cottages on the property were restored for guest use; one, an English-style 1930s bungalow, has become the hotel's health club. The historic Japanese and Horseshoe Gardens, along with a redwood picture bridge depicting forty-one hand-painted scenes of California, were carefully refurbished.

The design team set out to recreate the vigor of the Huntington, a storehouse of memories. In a two-year, fast-track program, the landmark hotel was totally transformed.

The design plan incorporates parking, building placement, and landscaping so that the old hotel remains integrated in the wealthy residential neighborhood of which it has long been a distinct and engaging part.

In a two-year, fast-track program, WAT&G set out to transform the 87-year-old Huntington Hotel from an outmoded, structurally-unsound facility to a five-star resort hotel equipped to meet every modern demand.

AERIAL VIEW

Several of the original historic features of the hotel were restored by the architects. An entry portal, recalling the original archway used for horse carriages, was reproduced to create a new entryway and lobby.

ENTRY VIEW

63

The elaborate, vaulted ceilings of the historic Georgia Room were repaired, and the roof of the vault was encapsulated with a new skin and completely reinforced with new footings for durability and safety.

In replicating the hotel's tower, all of the building's spaces, including many that had been unconventionally narrow, were reconfigured for improved flexibility and function.

To further integrate the old with the new, each addition takes an older architectural feature as its focal point. The new lobby lounge, bar, and grill all overlook historic gardens.

THE REGENT OF BANGKOK

When architect and client sat down together, both had visions of a new hotel in the tradition of legendary grand hotels of the Orient. Specifically, the goal in designing the Regent of Bangkok was to produce one of the finest hotels in Thailand, modern in every respect but also uniquely Thai. The hotel's design blends the styles of two worlds: the industrial world of efficiency and practicality and the Thai world of graciousness and tradition.

The design concept centers on a cluster of interconnecting buildings, a complex of individual units with the pure, soft lines of Thai houses but without the usual decorative Thai motifs. With simplicity of form and design in mind, a number of accomplished local artists were assembled to enrich the simple structures with sumptuous Thai art. The exterior is stately; a traditional Thai blue-tiled roof contrasts starkly with a gleaming white facade of plastered concrete. No attempt was made to copy the details of traditional Thai architecture. Instead, the design was made to retain grace and charm but have a functional approach.

At the entrance, a pair of handcarved sandstone elephants flank two lotus pools. The main entry is through a water court and a lobby of grand proportions, designed to combine a Western sense of worldly pleasure with the Eastern concept of eternity. Lobby columns — Doric squares with a simplified entablature — are of stark white plaster. The opulent ceiling is covered with intricate and symbolic Thai murals painted on silk. Behind the grand staircase, which leads from the lobby to small conference rooms on the mezzanine floor, a gigantic allegorical mural depicts the history of the kings of Thailand. The building's main core houses the lobby and reception areas, a formal dining room, and kitchens flanked by the open-air Parichart and Mouthathip courts. The Parichart Court is seven stories high, while the Mouthathip rises to eight; each was designed as a hollow rectangle with single-loaded corridors and room entryways facing a large, tropical garden.

The interior theme is a blend of the quieter elements of Western culture and the peace of Buddhism. On a symbolic level, a guest's arrival and progress through the primary rooms represents a spiritual journey that begins when visitors leave the noisy outside world and enter the quiet of the hotel: Moving from the image of the two royal elephants symbolizing earthly power, across the placid lotus ponds representative of the Buddhist concept of the emptiness of the after-death stage, into the lobby with its heavenly cosmos, and finally into the guest room, a world of gods and mythological and celestial beings.

LOCATION
Bangkok, Thailand

CLIENT
The Rajdamri Hotel Company

PROJECT SIZE
*387 guest rooms
(including 37 suites)*

AMENITIES
*4 restaurants; ballroom;
conference center;
business center; retail arcade;
swimming pool with cabanas;
rooftop tennis court;
sports and health club;
medical suite; 2 open-air atria
with courtyards; 2 squash courts;
beauty/barber shop*

Much of the Thai artwork that graces the hotel is intricately painted with glowing colors on silk panels.

Two open-air atria flank
the main building core,
and guest rooms open
onto either the seven-
story court or the eight-
story court. Greenery
spills down from each
floor to meet a rain
forest-like court divided
by a brook tumbling
across rocks from the
River Kwai.

A carefully blended selection of traditional Thai artworks and contemporary crafts of varied forms and styles subtly enrich the cool elegance of the hotel. This detail from a pair of carved temple doors depicts floral motifs and fierce guardian deities.

In the Parichart Court a waterfall, carp pool, and lush vegetation humanize the scale and soften the geometry of the seven-story building around them, creating an intimate and serene venue for al fresco dining.

As rustic and friendly as an old spice shop, the ground floor Spice Market restaurant presents authentic Thai cuisine in a setting patterned on the traditional Thai "shop-house", a building serving as both shop and living quarters. A brick and teak patterned floor and a hand-carved teak replica of the gateway to Chinatown's Thieves Market enliven the atmosphere.

Monumental scale defined by brilliant Doric columns sets the scene for the lobby's spectacular overhead panorama. Its ceiling of six richly adorned silk murals represents the Thai cosmos.

FOUR SEASONS HOTEL NEWPORT BEACH

THE CLIENT'S INTENT WAS TO build a 285-room luxury hotel which would give a vigorous identity to the retail and commercial complex of Fashion Island. A major challenge to the design team was to create a resort environment on a tight 4.5-acre urban site.

Envisioning the hotel as an urban oasis for the business and pleasure traveler, WAT&G set out to capture the essence of contemporary California architecture in the design of the Four Seasons Hotel Newport Beach.

The result is a 19-story guest tower whose dramatic silhouette stands in profile to Fashion Island. The angle of placement protects the views of nearby office buildings and homes and provides panoramic ocean views for 100 percent of the guest rooms. The tower's height allows space for an outdoor pool, tennis courts, terraces, and park-like landscaping. The pale, pre-cast concrete exterior echoes neighboring structures, while the vertical sweep of the sculpted, stepped-backed design adds a vital presence to the Newport Beach area. The hotel is distinctive without being distracting.

A cantilevered porte cochere adds to the drama of the contemporary design and gives guests an immediate sense of spaciousness. The tower's chamfered edges, the softening effect of landscaped niches at each tower elevation, terraced balconies, the private driveway entry off the main thoroughfare, and a spacious turn-around contribute to the idea of the hotel as a secluded retreat.

The lobby is airy and light — by design. Glass entry doors seem to float in space, an effect achieved by surrounding the doors with an architrave of cast stone which disguises the steel structure within. Floor-to-ceiling windows, ceiling detailing, and repetition of exterior art-deco motifs and octagonal incising bring a commodious outdoor feeling into the interiors, as do the landscaped terraces opening out from four major function rooms.

Each view was carefully considered. Since half the guest rooms look down on the ballroom roof, aluminum louvers treated with a protective finish to withstand sea air hide exhaust ducts. An adjacent roof was designed as an immense planter. Every element of the design of Four Seasons Hotel Newport Beach brings the outdoors inside, creating an oasis in the midst of a commercial center.

LOCATION
Newport Beach, California
USA

CLIENT
The Irvine Company

SITE SIZE
4.5 acres

PROJECT SIZE
344,270 square feet,
285 guest rooms
(including 93 suites)

AMENITIES
Health club;
3,000-square-foot pool;
2 tennis courts;
ballroom and
meeting facilities; spa

Twin sphinxes grace the entryway to the Four Seasons Hotel Newport Beach.

Views, reflections, use of color, and the repetition of shapes and motifs are all made part of a design which strengthens the relationship of indoor spaces to the exterior landscape.

*The boldly-sculptured
Four Seasons Hotel
Newport Beach gives a
vigorous identity to the
contemporary business/
retail complex of Fashion
Island. The design also
creates a resort-like
retreat within the con-
straints of an urban site.*

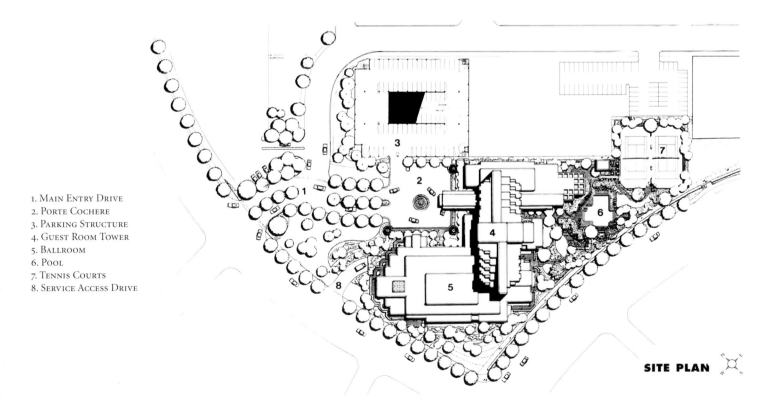

1. Main Entry Drive
2. Porte Cochere
3. Parking Structure
4. Guest Room Tower
5. Ballroom
6. Pool
7. Tennis Courts
8. Service Access Drive

SITE PLAN

Glass entries, spot lighting, and interior greenery
heighten the drama of
the lobby, which appears
to extend fluidly into the
out-of-doors.

Densely landscaped
terraces visible from
dining rooms and other
public areas of the hotel
enhance the effect of lush
oasis surroundings.

THE RITZ-CARLTON, LAGUNA NIGUEL

THE RESORT WHICH HAS BECOME the prototype for development of the Southern California coast began with design constrictions that appeared almost impossible to overcome.

The design program called for a world-class resort which would blend unobtrusively with its setting, a 150-foot-high natural bluff overlooking the Pacific. The hotel had to be large enough to fill all the expectations of a major international destination, but, as mandated by the California Coastal Commission, it could not be more than 185 feet in height.

The Ritz-Carlton, Laguna Niguel was the first major hotel built directly on the Southern California coast in thirty years. The client wanted it to offer an unparalleled sense of privacy and exclusivity to guests, but compliance with state and local building codes stipulated public access to the beach.

To meet these requirements, the architects chose Spanish Mediterranean style for the design. The simplicity of this style complements the bluffs and is typical of the Mission Period of Southern California, making it a suitable model for future building.

To give privacy to hotel guests and neighboring residents, the design forms an E with open legs extending away from the ocean. Two L-shaped wings of guest accommodations flank the central function area and shape spaces for gardens, swimming pool, and courtyards. These wings extend the sense of seclusion while offering a discreet public view from either side and from the beachfront. Public access to the historic surfers' haven of Salt Creek Beach is behind the parking area and along a sheltered promontory.

Height restrictions were turned to advantages. Design plans modified the typical Spanish-style hip roof to hide mechanical systems within a well under the cut-off peak. The first floor was situated fifteen feet below existing grade with the excavated sand used to form additional beach.

Overall, the architectural objective was simplicity. The French doors and windows were sized to complement the architecture without sacrificing the view of the ocean. Colors and materials were understated to blend with the natural setting. From the ocean, The Ritz-Carlton, Laguna Niguel appears to be some intriguing Mediterranean village, melded to the bluff, that has grown there slowly over time.

LOCATION
Dana Point, California
USA

CLIENT
W. B. Johnson Properties, Inc.

SITE SIZE
17.5 acres

PROJECT SIZE
330,000 square feet,
393 guest rooms

AMENITIES
4 tennis courts;
2 heated pools;
fitness center;
18-hole golf course;
2 miles of beachfront

The Ritz-Carlton, Laguna Niguel's extraordinary location on a bluff high over the Pacific Ocean — with a view of the Catalina Island and miles of coastline — governed design plans for the site.

Classic interior lines make a restrained backdrop for the large display of valuable art and antiques that are trademarks of the hotel.

To give a rather large property residential scale and a feeling of seclusion, interior spaces are divided into comfortable, intimate settings.

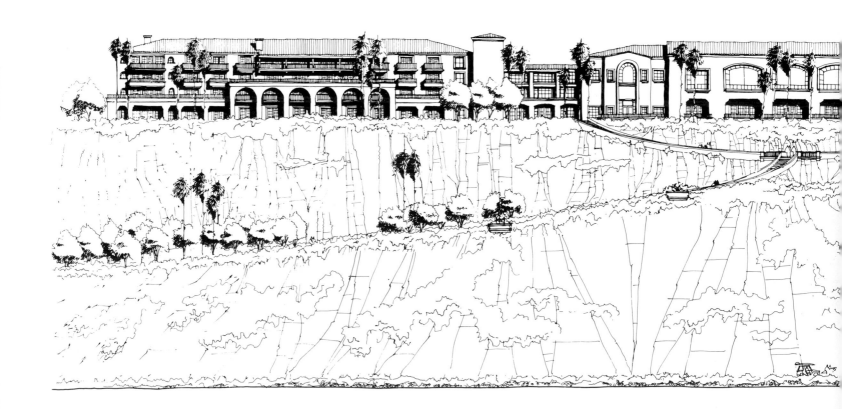

The architectural design focuses on quality, restraint, and compatibility with the setting: The ocean is always a focal point for this design.

A columned promenade, echoing the classic proportions of the facade, extends from the hotel entrance to ocean views.

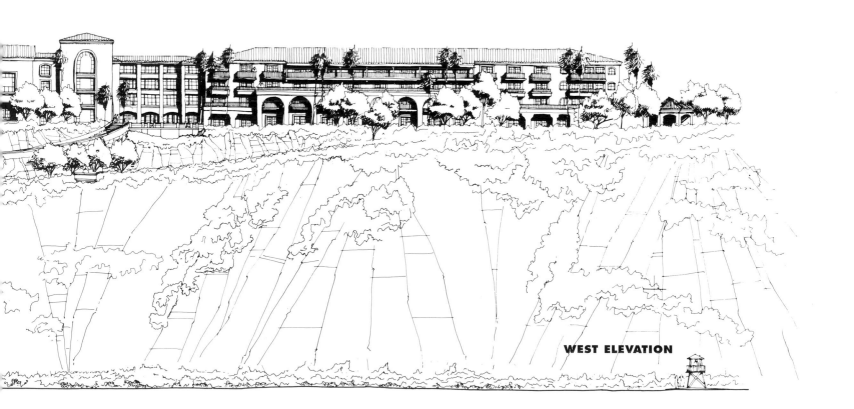

WEST ELEVATION

THE PALACE OF THE LOST CITY

LOCATION
*Republic of Bophuthatswana
South Africa
(100 miles northwest
of Johannesburg)*

CLIENT
*Sol Kerzner, Chairman,
Sun International, Ltd.*

SITE SIZE
68 acres

PROJECT SIZE
*580,000 square feet,
350 guest rooms*

AMENITIES
*21 suites; 6 restaurants;
Olympic-size pool;
water adventure park;
17 acres of lakes,
rivers and jungles;
two 18-hole Gary Player
golf courses and other
recreational facilities;
casino gaming*

IN THE MIDST OF A VOLCANIC crater one hundred miles from the nearest urban center, the charge from the client was this: Design a luxury hotel of unprecedented opulence and originality that will lure the most sophisticated traveler.

The area was technologically primitive; the site was unremarkable. To add to the initial challenge, the client wanted the project completed in under 32 months from start of design to grand opening.

The challenge was met first with a literary blueprint. This fictional narrative, devised by the design architect, tells of a nomadic North African tribe who settled in this arid southern region and built a magnificent palace and city. Their new architecture mingled faded memories of turrets, domes, and arches from their past with the lush fauna and flora of their new home. In the legend, an earthquake destroys the village but leaves the palace largely intact, awaiting discovery.

This story became a design tool, and the architects set out to recreate an architecture that had never really existed. To ground this nebulous concept in reality, the WAT&G team followed three self-imposed dictates:

The Palace would be designed first as a palace, second as a hotel. The storehouse to be mined for concept and decorative elements was the lore of southern Africa. And The Palace would be a serious project that would respect the regional environment.

The myth shaped both the appearance and the function of The Palace. The story called for breathtaking scale, so the 85-foot-high lobby-rotunda is conceived as the royal entrance chamber. This rotunda and the adjacent Crystal Court form a two-level core housing public spaces.

All design elements of The Palace — from its site on the highest point in the landscape, and its magnitude of scale, to the almost 15,000 pieces of precast custom-made ornamentation — were planned and built to complete the effect of a venture into a newly-discovered world. Over 100 forms of natural vegetation and wildlife — the textures of leaf patterns, the shapes of protea blossoms — adorn facades and archways; the animals of the veldt — elephant and kudo, monkey and crane — ornament towers and ceilings. This richness of detail creates a constant sense of Africa and of a mystical, distant past. Now completed, and seemingly 1,000 years old, The Palace of The Lost City tells its own story.

A *fictional account of a mythical lost kingdom, newly rediscovered, became the basis of the design, and all public areas, council rooms, and guest accommodations carry out the theme. A constant sense of movement is captured in sculpted animal forms and in the lines of arches incised with native flora.*

Water, used as an architectural feature, frames The Palace which seems to rise from the surrounding lake. Vast arches and columns create changes of light, shadow, and color on the water, and their reflections add variety and intrigue to the setting.

The drama of The Palace, surrounded by water and approached across a graceful entrance bridge, is emphasized at night by lighting from the ten towers.

Animal forms, transitional elements between the slender tower and the domes, are molded as gargoyle-like images from glass-fiber reinforced concrete.

The design team spent
hundreds of hours
sketching various compo-
nents of The Palace and
devising ways to merge
diverse elements —
everything from footing
and stairs to lamps and
animal sculptures —
into a cohesive design.

Cast-bronze light fixtures
used in the landscape
ceremonial areas com-
bine gas flames in the
upper flame bowl and
concealed incandescent
up-lighting reflecting off
the bowl bottom. All the
light appears to come
from a natural flame.

The architects undertook
a series of studies to
devise patterns which
would unify The Palace.
The bundling of reeds
and arching palm-fronds
are a natural reference to
the early architecture of
an ancient people.

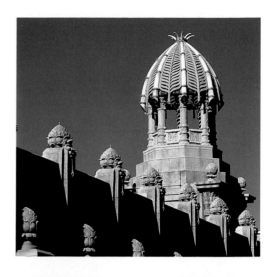
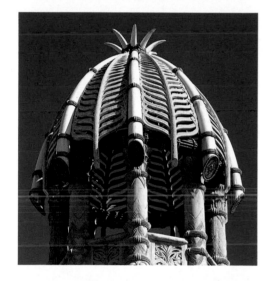

In every monumental feature and in every minute detail, The Palace is designed to replicate an ancient and mythical royal residence of unprecedented opulence and originality.

Guest rooms open to a five-story space crowned by a skylit ceiling supported by structural stone columns and accented with simulated tusk mullions.

A six-story rotunda graces the main entry and features a hand-painted jungle scene above and a hand-laid marble mosaic floor below.

Throughout the project, the fantasy concept has been conveyed in intricate, baroque detail derived from the vigor of southern Africa.

The use of native plant forms and patterns is a unifying element in both interior and exterior architectural design. Floral representations are often grandly scaled to create drama and movement.

CHEJU SHILLA HOTEL

LOCATION
Cheju Island, Korea

CLIENT
*The Shilla Hotel Company
(Samsung Group)*

SITE SIZE
21 acres

PROJECT SIZE
*330 rooms
(including 12 Korean rooms
and 20 suites; 100 rooms in
Phase 2 expansion)*

AMENITIES
*3 restaurants;
library bar; casino;
duty-free shop; fitness club;
indoor/outdoor pool;
six-lane bowling alley*

IT IS NATURAL TO ASSUME that a resort hotel in Korea would feature architectural motifs indigenous to Korea, so that foreigners could have a "Korean" experience while staying at the hotel. That was not the case with the 330-room Cheju Shilla Hotel, however, which was designed to appeal mainly to the domestic market.

The client's intent was to bring something exotic to the local guests — in particular, Southern Californian Mediterranean-style architecture, with its stucco walls, arched windows and portals, terra cotta tile roofs, and reinforced concrete structure. It is a style WAT&G previously employed in its design for The Ritz-Carlton, Laguna Niguel and one which greatly impressed the Korean client.

Behind the California-Spanish style in Cheju is a hotel that offers Koreans a Western vacation experience but easily accommodates traditional Korean customs. Three large banquet rooms were created for large weddings, which are traditional in Korea. (This is a very popular honeymoon hotel.) A mechanically operated glass door separates the indoor and outdoor pools and shields guests from the temperature fluctuations common on Cheju Island.

The entire complex was designed and engineered to withstand the island's periodic typhoons.

Public spaces within the hotel are large enough to accommodate the planned addition of 100 guest rooms. To create more intimately-scaled spaces within the hotel's large lobby, the architect designed oversized, glass screen-tile block dividing walls. Enhancing the visual interest in the lower lobby is a custom-made skylight which provides natural light to the indoor pool below it.

A multi-cultural blend is evident in the hotel's interior design and even in the mix of restaurants: Korean, Japanese, and Western. With architectural design coming from the U.S., construction skills from Korea, and interior design from a firm in France, this hotel is truly an international venture.

Designed to offer its guests a complete and luxurious vacation experience, the complex includes a fitness club, a duty-free shop, a casino, a bowling alley, conference facilities, Korean and Western-style guest rooms, and an 18-hole golf course. Extensive landscaping on the lush, 21-acre site includes a waterfall and several lagoons.

All in all, it's a place for Koreans to get away and find relaxation without having to travel very far.

An exterior stair with classic balustrade descends in a long, graceful curve from the upper lobby terrace to the lower lobby and outdoor dining terrace. Red tile steps complement the red tile roof.

Designed — at the client's request — to provide a California-style vacation experience for Korean guests, Cheju Shilla exhibits signature elements of Spanish and Mediterranean influenced Santa Barbara architecture: a terra cotta tile roof, stucco walls, and arched windows and portals.

The spaciousness of the California-style sunlit lobby accommodates traditional Korean customs: Public spaces and function areas must comfortably hold the masses of people associated with Korean weddings.

Arriving guests enter a central core which radiates to four wings, each with five stories. The central building — with lobby, restaurants and bar, health club, swimming pool, and bowling alley — presides over golf course and ocean vistas.

89

THE PRIMARY GOAL IN THE remodeling of the Sheraton Harbor Island Resort was to greatly improve the hotel's level of quality and services in the San Diego marketplace. The client asked WAT&G to create an attraction for major business and trade show conferees, that would also offer vacationing families the atmosphere and amenities of a sophisticated resort.

SHERATON HARBOR ISLAND RESORT

The hotel facility, originally built in 1972, had been through a series of renovations over the years. As a result, its image was unclear and its public spaces were outmoded. The design team and the client agreed on three directives: (1) The hotel would be remodeled to exemplify San Diego as it is today — a vibrant, friendly, and cosmopolitan harbor city. (2) The design would focus attention on the very engaging bay location. (3) Additions and reconfigurations would eliminate confusing traffic patterns.

First, the exterior of the resort was changed. The architects added a new drive, a fountain, and a porte cochere. The exterior was also repainted for a brighter look.

The lobby and adjoining public areas were greatly enlarged by tearing out walls and raising ceilings; minor infrastructure was relocated where necessary. To add light and views, spaces were expanded out towards the bay: a newly-created curving window-wall frames a view of the entire marina.

The creation of a trompe l'oeil ceiling above a stylized cherry-wood trellis gave the lobby added drama. The lines of the trellis create an almost forced perspective by appearing to converge at the harbor view.

The three original dining areas were replaced with a single, multi-level dining area that seats 400. The view faces directly west. To control sunlight and regulate environmental conditions, automatic, motorized shades were installed. The shades, which are double-paned and heat resistant, are translucent and untinted to allow for true rendition of color.

The remodeled Sheraton Harbor Island Resort reflects the modern city of San Diego and its spectacular harbor location. The transformation is so dramatic that visitors often mistake the resort for a brand new property.

LOCATION
*San Diego, California
USA*

CLIENT
ITT Sheraton Corporation

SITE SIZE
15 acres

PROJECT SIZE
22,540 square feet of new facilities (and 149,000 square feet of renovated space), 1,048 guest rooms (including renovation of 700-room East Tower)

AMENITIES
Executive conference center; pool area and spa; waterfalls; 80-seat pool restaurant and bar

The hotel's new design is aimed at enhancing and highlighting the property's outdoor amenities.

To reorient the public areas towards the marina, the renovation project shifted the axis of the entry lobby from the front door and expanded it towards the harbor. The lines of a new cherry wood trellis on the lobby ceiling lead toward and accentuate the bay view.

The renovation of the Sheraton Harbor Island Resort completely reconfigured the hotel's entry drive. Additions to the exterior included extensive tropical landscaping, a dramatic fountain, a new porte cochere, and an arched cap addition on the tower.

The design expands public spaces toward the bay and uses pools, landscaping, and boardwalks to link the hotel to its vibrant setting.

THE DESIGN FOCUS FOR THIS Four Seasons hotel is a wonderful 17-acre park laid out in 1877 by Prince Aritomo Yamagata near the center of metropolitan Tokyo. The park's romantic and historic gardens, which provide a foreground to the hotel, hold deep meaning for the people of Japan and are a favored setting for wedding ceremonies. Two primary goals of the client were to offer a hotel environment of unrivaled refinement and elegance that would complement a Japanese tradition of elaborate wedding celebrations, and to offer guests an atmosphere of serenity in the midst of a frenetic city.

FOUR SEASONS HOTEL CHINZAN-SO

Using the garden as a symbol of what the design should be, the architects developed a plan conducive to quiet and relaxation throughout the hotel property.

Because of the limited three-acre footprint, the design takes a vertical approach with a 13-story tower. The contemporary exterior, with its angularity and huge expanses of faceted glass, opens public areas and guest rooms to the gardens.

A more traditional, "Western" design characterizes the interior and emphasizes spaciousness with a sense of seclusion. A dramatic enclosed pool, developed in a former backyard delivery area, has a barrel vault roof which opens to let in natural light and air. This conservatory-like spa, sequestered within its own private garden, provides a natural, peaceful respite.

Public spaces, positioned on several levels, include a wedding chapel, photo studio, bridal shrine, dressing room for wedding participants, florist, an eclectic array of restaurants, and over 26,000 square feet of banquet and meeting rooms capable of accommodating as many as 1,000 or as few as 8 individuals. Each is designed to preserve the privacy of its guests.

The intimate, residential atmosphere of the hotel's entry-level public spaces results from a planned progression. A rather large lobby opens to a smaller lounge which leads to a series of smaller public areas overlooking the tranquil gardens.

This hotel, Four Seasons' first venture in Asia, expresses the ancient Japanese belief that fortune will shine on those who situate themselves in harmony with the natural landscape.

LOCATION
Tokyo, Japan

CLIENT
*Fujita Tourist
Enterprises Co., Ltd.*

SITE SIZE
17 acres

PROJECT SIZE
*380,000 square feet,
286 guest rooms*

AMENITIES
*16 conference rooms;
100-seat amphitheater;
business center; spa;
shops and gallery;
wedding facilities*

Designed to be a haven from stress, the fitness center features a luxurious onsen *bath with natural mineral water from the famous Itoh hot springs.*

The state-of-the-art spa facility mixes contemporary with classical: the lines of columns and arches stand in relief against the modern roof and sunlit pool.

The architectural design of the hotel joins Eastern and Western traditions to create a quiet, intimate atmosphere in interior spaces.

Subtle lighting and natural wood ceilings are designed to blend the interior of the hotel with the historic and honored Japanese garden that is an important part of both the site and the overall architectural design.

Portions of the hotel's interior design have a distinctly Japanese flavor, while the exterior takes a contemporary, high-rise approach to comply with strict site limitations.

It took audacity to undertake redevelopment of the city block that became Hyatt Regency Waikiki; both the high cost of land and the high cost of credit cast doubt on the project's economic feasibility. Two things were critical to making the project work: retail space and an accelerated design and construction process.

To make the retail component economi-

HYATT REGENCY WAIKIKI

cally viable, the design plan required 80,000 square feet of space. There was insufficient space at street level to meet this requirement. The solution was a three-story podium which provided room for 70 retail shops. Because multi-level shopping centers have no history of

success in Hawaii, the architect devised a circulation pattern that sent hotel guests circuitously past shops at upper levels.

At the time of its construction, Hyatt Waikiki earned the distinction of having the biggest mortgage in Hawaii history. This resulted in an interest rate of more than $1,000 an hour. Thus, delays and cost overruns were serious matters. Valuable time was saved through a negotiated fast-track contract. The excavation and foundation work were started, for example, before the drawings for most of the building interiors were completed. Communication and cooperation were vital components of the process to ensure that the flow of drawings and data from architect to contractor meshed with the construction schedule.

LOCATION
*Waikiki Beach – Honolulu
Oahu, Hawaii
USA*

CLIENT
*Christopher B. Hemmeter
Hemmeter Development Corp.*

SITE SIZE
*One city block;
104,455 square feet*

PROJECT SIZE
*Twin towers, 40 stories each;
1,260 rooms and suites*

AMENITIES
*70 retail shops
(80,000 square feet);
94,000-square-foot conference
center; swimming pool;
3-story open air atrium
with monumental sculpture;
2 presidential suites; 8 penthouse
suites; 68 tower suites*

The landscaping design provides tropical ambience and sound-masking devices, but goes beyond the obvious to create a sense of human scale in the block-long, ten-story atrium that connects Hyatt Regency Waikiki's two 40-story towers.

From both towers, grand stairs clad in brass and fine wood descend elegantly into the street-cafe atmosphere of the "Great Hall," which serves as a resort focal point. Seventy shops and restaurants on three landscaped levels add to the "holiday mood" and economically justify the amount of space left open in this 450-foot-long open mall.

In choosing an octagonal twin-tower configuration rather than a single, less costly room block, the architects decreased guest room count but increased the number of ocean-view rooms. The solution also preserves a wide view corridor between the buildings, lessening environmental impact.

THE RITZ-CARLTON HOTEL Company's first Hawaiian property benefited from a large 32-acre site on the Big Island's Kohala coast, with no neighbors on either side and excellent views of the ocean and golf course. The architectural approach was to create a residential scale and a serene atmosphere in a 542-room hotel within the master-planned Mauna Lani Resort.

THE RITZ-CARLTON, MAUNA LANI

At the turn of the century, Hawaii was influenced by the classical architecture of the mainland, which had, in turn, been influenced by European classical design. The architecture of The Ritz-Carlton, Mauna Lani, in its openness, proportions, and atmosphere, blends Hawaii's European and native traditions.

The overall style of the hotel gives the appearance of an estate or grand European villa; much of the detailing is native Hawaiian. The double-pitched roofs, colored tiles, and regional motifs, such as the large sculpted pineapples used as anchoring posts for stairwells, reflect this heritage.

Because of the favorable climate, a primary feature throughout the hotel is the relationship of indoors to outdoors, as seen in folding doors and windows that open to the exterior. In spaces away from dominant winds, the design takes advantage of ocean breezes or natural ventilation. Balconies have six feet of overhang and protect most openings from direct sunlight — providing energy conservation and giving guests outdoor enjoyment accessible from their rooms.

The typical length of stay on the island — six days is average — was also a consideration. Interior courtyards open to the sky to offer guests a variety of spatial experiences. Restaurants and lounges are diverse in style and placement.

The orientation of public spaces toward views, especially views of the Kohala coast, the Pacific, and the pool, helps provide a constant sense of discovery.

On the site, the design team created a very natural-looking swimming lagoon and white sand beach without disrupting the character of the lava and coral formation of the coastline. An ancient Hawaiian saltwater fishpond was preserved as a micro-climate for marine life and has become a notable, attractive feature adding to the resort's appeal.

LOCATION
*South Kohala Coast, Hawaii
USA*

CLIENT
*The Ritz-Carlton
Hotel Company*

SITE SIZE
32 acres

PROJECT SIZE
542 guest rooms

AMENITIES
*White sand beach and
protected ocean lagoon;
10,000-square-foot swimming pool;
11 tennis courts, including
an exhibition court;
18-hole golf course;
fitness center;
7 restaurants;
conference facilities*

The use of residential scale and traditional European proportions, along with creative grading of the landscape, minimizes the visual impact of the hotel. The structure appears serene, suitable to the landscape, and smaller than its six-stories.

Fusion of Hawaii's European and native traditions in the architectural style of the hotel gives The Ritz-Carlton, Mauna Lani, a strong identity; the overall design resembles that of a European estate, while design details, such as koa wood banisters, are distinctly Hawaiian.

Double-pitched roofs with broad overhangs emphasize the residential scale of the resort; the large cantilever at the top floors and throughout the main building conserves energy by providing shade and offering protection from rain.

Taking full advantage of Hawaii's year-round hospitable climate, the architect created interior courtyards that are open to the sky.

To provide a variety of experiences for guests, The Ritz-Carlton, Mauna Lani offers abundant recreational amenities, including a protected saltwater lagoon and 11 lighted tennis courts.

LEISURE PROJECTS

BROKEN TOP

First, the program called for a residentially scaled building to house administrative, marketing, sales, and accounting staff for the 500-acre, master-planned development of Broken Top residential resort in central Oregon. This structure — with its copper roof, stone forms, and prominent use of wood — sets the tone for the design of other homes within the community.

The second program-component is a golf clubhouse that serves as a private 18-hole championship golf course. The client asked that it be architecturally significant and versatile enough to function as a winter-sports clubhouse during snow season. The clubhouse was also designed as an inviting living room on a grand scale for the Broken Top community. In addition, both the clubhouse and the information center are made to be compatible with the ruggedly picturesque setting.

The clubhouse appears rooted to a prominent, boulder- and brush-covered plateau with 360-degree exposure to the community. The design is organized by the dramatic placement of two massive cross-axial walls constructed of stone quarried and cut on-site. These walls align with the earth's cardinal points; one is laid directly north to south, the other east to west. Visually striking, they anchor and impart permanence to the building. Enclosing the four quadrants created by the stone walls is a structural framework of wood trusses, glass, and an aged-copper roof.

The greatroom of the clubhouse was designed to be the heart of the community throughout the year. Exposed cedar trusses support high ceilings; expansive glass allows views of the nearby volcanic peaks of the Cascade Mountains. A terrace just outside the greatroom overlooks the five-acre lake in the foreground and expands the opportunity to enjoy pleasant weather. A massive, free-standing fireplace rising thirty feet through the ceiling and roof is a convivial cold-weather gathering place.

The grandeur of the surrounding landscape is reflected even in the staircase, which has been created from natural boulders shaped like huge sculpted forms. Cedar stairs descend over and through the boulders, and one forms the base of the main fireplace.

LOCATION
*Bend, Oregon
USA*

CLIENT
Broken Top, Inc.

SITE SIZE
500 acres

PROJECT SIZE
25,000 square feet

AMENITIES
*18-hole golf course; pro shop;
locker room; exercise room;
swimming complex;
public dining areas;
members' grill;
retreat for winter skiers*

The vigorous relationship of site, materials, and structure in the design of Broken Top recalls the architectural style of Frank Lloyd Wright.

Broken Top's design complements the rugged beauty of its setting and is structured to afford panoramic vistas of the lake, golf course, and forest land in the distance.

The clubhouse — designed as the heart of the Broken Top resort's 500 acres — serves as a year-round gathering place.

The architectural character of the information center echoes that of the clubhouse. Together they set the tone for the design of the entire resort.

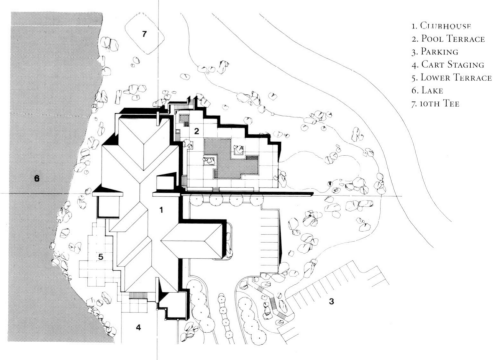

1. CLUBHOUSE
2. POOL TERRACE
3. PARKING
4. CART STAGING
5. LOWER TERRACE
6. LAKE
7. 10TH TEE

SITE PLAN

PARKROYAL SHOPPING VILLAGE, CAIRNS INTERNATIONAL

FROM ITS STATELY COLUMNS and white latticework to its windows reaching three stories high, this resort hotel and accompanying shopping village looks the way most international visitors to North Queensland would expect. A thorough study of the region — its history, culture, climate, and design — resulted in the choice of Victorian Colonial architecture, a style that was very much a part of Far Northern Queensland, and yet one that was disappearing rapidly.

Translating this style into contemporary buildings (including a highrise) was accomplished through the details: sculpted wrought-iron railings and timber lattice-work, spindles, and brackets. These elements were actually adaptations of the English Colonial style that was transported to Australia from the British colonies. Instead of strictly recreating a period (which might have resulted in a dark and overly sentimental effect), the architects and interior designers sought to capture its essence.

The five-star hotel features comprehensive convention facilities which appeal to the business market, as well as restaurants, spas, two lagoon pools, and a themed retail village, which appeal to visitors and local residents alike. The shopping village's 54 specialty boutique shops are as distinguished as their turn-of-the-century Victorian detailing; both have workmanship seldom seen in contemporary architecture.

Landscaping and low-rise buildings invite pedestrians to explore the informal charm of the shopping village, with its old-style Queensland shops, restaurants, and galleries. The fine, intimate, residential-style appointments of the shopping village were brought into the interiors of the hotel's vast public areas, thereby providing this conference/destination resort hotel with the atmosphere of a smaller, boutique hotel.

Perhaps the ultimate compliment came near completion of the Victorian style, newly built project. An elderly gentleman of Cairns strolled by and exclaimed, "Isn't it wonderful that they're saving all the old buildings around here!"

LOCATION
*Cairns, Queensland
Australia*

CLIENT
Solander Industries Pty. Ltd.

SITE SIZE
2 acres

PROJECT SIZE
*321 rooms,
54 shops in retail village*

AMENITIES
*Large convention facility
with 10 meeting rooms
and banquet space; three-
quarter-acre tropical pool
and entertainment area;
3 spas; Colonial-
theme retail village*

The Abbott Street entry of the hotel tower expresses the Colonial Queensland theme architecturally through its use of arches, columns, balustrades, shutters, and a veranda-like porte cochere.

For twenty-first century hotel guests, nineteenth century Victorian architecture must be lightened up. The architect called for the discreet use of selected, period elements. Dark wood suggests the period elegantly and authentically while stately columns, soaring windows, a three-story lobby, and informal furnishings make Cairns International hotel inviting and comfortable.

The low-rise buildings and informal landscaping invite pedestrians to stroll among meandering paths, seek the shade of canopied and latticed verandas, and explore the old-style Queensland shops, galleries, and restaurants.

Distinctive features typifying turn-of-the-century Cairns define the shopping village, which is a full block wide and has access from two streets.

Far from being a superimposed design gimmick, the return to the graceful, well-crafted facades and verandas of Colonial Cairns helps preserve a vernacular architecture and remains outback-practical in tropical Queensland's hot, humid climate.

PRINCIPE FELIPE, HYATT LA MANGA CLUB

CALLED A "CONTEMPORARY CASTLE" by some, this five-star resort had a much more modest start. It is actually the outgrowth of an existing, mid-market, 47-room hotel that was more of a golf clubhouse with accommodations than a full-service resort. Unfortunately, the original 1970s Modernist building had been constructed of reinforced concrete and built to last. Rather than tear it down and start over, the architects stripped it to its structural basics, then renovated and expanded from there.

The challenge was to transform the outdated facility into a deluxe, Andalusian-style resort that would attract leisure guests, golfers, families, and business travelers. To design a resort that was both classic and contemporary, the architects drew from motifs found in historic Spanish villas of the early 18th century: arches, arcades, wrought iron railings, terra cotta roofs, and exposed terraces.

The resort now features spacious guest rooms, a large selection of dining facilities, and an impressive range of recreation options, including: three 18-hole championship golf courses, an 18-court tennis center, a gymnasium, spa, beach club, equestrian center, and more. (La Manga now serves as the base for the Professional Golfers Association of Europe.) All of the amenities are available not only to hotel guests but also to residents of the resort's 72 on-site apartments.

Providing leading-edge leisure facilities and making those facilities accessible from the hotel was essential. The designers re-oriented the building and reconfigured the interior space to showcase these leisure facilities and to encourage guests to try them out. All of the guest rooms now have a sweeping view of the surrounding golf course; the hotel's public spaces have terraces that provide a direct visual and physical link to the recreational activities.

Designed to attract upscale business year-round by giving its guests the royal treatment, the Hotel Principe Felipe actually derives its name from Spain's Prince Felipe, a frequent visitor to La Manga who agreed to lend his name to the resort.

LOCATION
Cartagena, Murcia
Spain

CLIENT
Bovis Abroad Limited

SITE SIZE
1,400 acres

PROJECT SIZE
200 rooms, 6 suites,
a royal suite, 72 apartments

AMENITIES
Three 18-hole
championship golf courses;
18-court tennis center;
gymnasium and spa;
beach club; soccer field;
crown green bowling;
equestrian center; jazz bar

Through an extensive program of renovation and expansion, the architects dramatically transformed an austere hotel and golf club into a colorfully detailed expression of classic Spain.

114 PRINCIPE FELIPE, HYATT LA MANGA CLUB

The Jazz Bar — serving food, drink, and live music — features locally-crafted, contemporary Spanish lighting fixtures, sculpted wrought iron, and hand-painted ceramics.

Arches, arcades, railings, and other interior motifs were inspired by the traditional designs found in 18th-century Spanish villas.

The Principe Felipe, Hyatt La Manga Club's public spaces all have terraces that provide a direct visual link to recreational facilities.

The lobby's high, vaulted ceiling, stone floor, and white walls suggest the entry hall of an old villa, with contemporary interpretations of that era evident in the selection of fixtures and furnishings.

GRAND HYATT BALI, GALLERIA RETAIL/ CULTURAL CENTRE

LOCATION
Nusa Dua, Bali
Indonesia

CLIENT
P.T. Wynncor Bali

SITE SIZE
40 acres (hotel), 27 acres
(retail/cultural complex)

PROJECT SIZE
750 guest rooms in four clusters,
including 35 suites and 4
deluxe villas; 248,000-square-
foot retail/cultural complex

AMENITIES
Indonesian food court;
ethnic dining options;
fitness center; tennis courts;
squash courts; beach club;
3 swimming pools;
retail/cultural complex;
business center;
conference facilities

ONE OF THE GREATEST challenges in designing this 750-room, full-service luxury resort and retail complex was to do so without overwhelming the terrain and culture of its location — the beautiful and exotic island of Bali.

WAT&G found design inspiration in the Balinese village. Buildings are organized into four decentralized clusters with their own courtyards, creating a more intimate scale for guests and visitors. Each cluster features a separate theme, and all are connected by lighted, landscaped pathways to the main lobby village.

None of the structures rises higher than four stories, thereby adhering to the local edict that no building shall exceed the height of a coconut tree (15m). The Balinese double-pitched clay roofs with generous overhanging eaves help establish the architectural character of the hotel.

An expansive waterfront site allowed for the amenities of this resort to be spread among the landscaped grounds. Hotel guests can wander the gardens, past a lavish array of pools, waterfalls, and lagoons, which together capture the essence of the Balinese water palace. The sounds and sights of water, integral to the design, enrich the visitor's experience.

With restaurants dispersed throughout the site, guests can choose from a wide choice of cuisines (Chinese, Japanese, Balinese, Malaysian, Italian, European); each is housed in a structure that reflects a different ethnic style. Or visitors can stroll in the Pasar Senggol, modeled after the festive Balinese open-air street markets, complete with food outlets, boutiques, a theater, and even a Hindu temple which the architects preserved in its original location.

A large convention center on-site serves Bali's business visitors, while a full range of sports facilities — swimming pools, a fitness club, and a gymnasium — meet the recreational needs of travelers.

The Galleria Retail/Cultural Centre attracts visitors to its garden setting and offers them a cultural shopping experience. Much more than a shopping mall, the cultural aspects of the retail complex include craft demonstrations in village-like settings and an amphitheater which features Balinese-inspired performances and exhibits. A relatively simple design — reinforced concrete structure with a stucco finish and clay-tiled roof — allowed for the buildings' rapid construction.

Within the complex, larger structures, such as the department stores, resemble Balinese ruins, while smaller shops are modeled after Balinese row-houses. Strategically placed courtyards serve as gathering places for visitors.

A study in compatible contrasts — active and serene, vast and intimate — this resort was designed to suit the island of Bali and the diversity of its visitors.

The resort helps sustain
traditional Balinese
culture with botanical
research performed on-
site and landscaping
programs that incorpo-
rate native jungle plants.

Lily ponds and pools are
kept clean by a biological
filtering system using fish,
rather than chemicals.

Carved wooden doors grace the entrance to the Watercourt Cafe. They are flanked by guardian statues and a split gate sculpted of local stone.

The lobby/reception building derives its architectural character from the Balinese water palace. The flagstone entry colonnade is surrounded by lotus ponds.

Ornamental gates serve as a backdrop for Balinese-inspired performances at the Galleria Retail/Cultural Centre.

The use of local materials and indigenous architectural motifs conveys both a sense of authenticity and intimacy.

The successful integration of native style and Western standards can be seen in the interiors, which feature Indonesian carvings, local materials, and Balinese art.

IN TURN-OF-THE-CENTURY America, millionaires from what Southerners called *up North* traveled annually to the seaside resorts of Florida. These hotel havens offered balmy respite from harsh winters and city life. Could those golden days live again at a grand hotel designed to offer every modern comfort?

The Disney Development Company

DISNEY'S© GRAND FLORIDIAN BEACH RESORT

called on WAT&G for practical answers. The client requested a spirited re-creation of the Victorian era in a 900-room world class resort hotel. The magic of the design had to function in the context of the world renowned destination, Walt Disney World.

The design team decided to take an interpretive approach to the architecture. Traveling through central Florida, Key West, and the Southeast, the architects located reference sources in libraries and in the field. Resort hotels of the era from the Caribbean to California were scrutinized.

Throughout the resulting design, l9th-century charm emerges through the use of 20th-century ingenuity and knowledge.

The original site plan called for 750 rooms; when the number changed to 900, the architects' solution fit cozy attic guest rooms behind what originally had been conceived as false dormers. To create a comfortable atmosphere in an immense hotel, the buildings are arranged village-style and limited to five stories.

Faced with an existing monorail system that had to meld with the main building, the team designed a Victorian-style train station as the hotel entry and porte cochere. An arcaded bridge leads to the hotel's atrium lobby. This grand lobby, designed as a five-story atrium with a themed elevator and three stained glass, back-lit domes, is the heart of the hotel.

To provide easy maintenance and meet fire and safety requirements, fiberglass cast from wooden Victorian models is used for most grillwork, brackets, and posts. However, items guests might touch or observe at close range are wood.

Aluminum siding, which covers most exterior walls, is also designed to replicate wood. The external fire escape has a clapboard shield and pitched roof.

Disney's Grand Floridian Beach Resort is a thematic rendering of huge dimensions in which every detail is carefully thought out to create a seamless fantasy.

LOCATION
Walt Disney World
Lake Buena Vista, Florida
USA

CLIENT
Disney Development
Company

SITE SIZE
40 acres

PROJECT SIZE
772,558 square feet,
900 rooms

AMENITIES
Monorail station;
7 restaurants and lounges;
health club; spa;
8,000-square-foot pool;
2 tennis courts; snack bar;
arcade; child-care facility;
marina; retail shops;
conference facilities;
wedding chapel

The visitor steps from the futuristic monorail into a Victorian train station designed as entry/ porte cochere and walks through an arcaded bridge into the grand entrance of the main building.

The 900-room Grand
Floridian is a re-creation
of the Victorian era ren-
dered in an impressionistic
architectural style which
draws from stylized
Victoriana suitable to a
tropical environment.

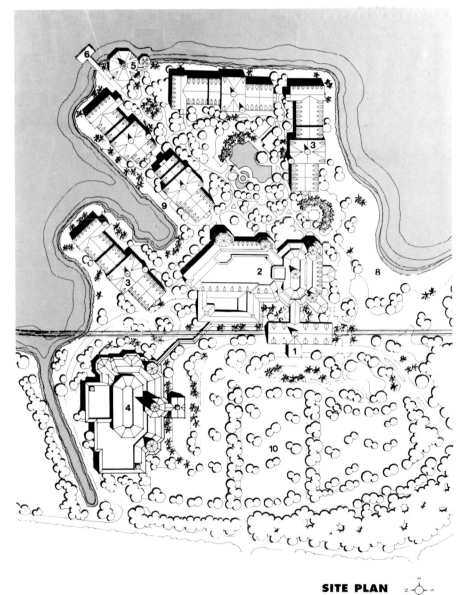

1. PORTE COCHERE
2. MAIN BUILDING
3. LODGE
4. CONFERENCE FACILITIES
5. SEAFOOD RESTAURANT
6. DOCK
7. POOL
8. BEACH
9. MARINA
10. PARKING

SITE PLAN

For fire safety, fiberglass replicates wood for most grillwork, brackets, and posts. Wherever guests might touch or observe surfaces at close range, such as stairways and banisters in the atrium lobby, wood is used.

In the historic district of Temecula, California, known as Old Town, a Western-themed plan uses Temecula's past to create a resort destination. The project objective was to develop a dynamic Old Town commercial and residential core while respecting Temecula's historic buildings.

To achieve this goal, every aspect of the development was masterplanned, from the small store-front, pedestrian-oriented design (as might have occurred at the turn of the century) to the development of consistent streetscape and architectural palettes. Streets, parking areas, and walkways are softened with decomposed granite or wooden planking; wind-resistant, drought-tolerant native plants are used in informal landscaping as a reference to rustic, early California settlements.

The proposed entertainment complex fully integrates with these guidelines and with existing Old Town buildings. The complex is designed to capture a large audience of visitors and to revitalize economic

growth for Temecula and Riverside County.

The first phase of buildings in Old Town Temecula includes a Wild West arena that seats 4,800; a full-scale, 2,200-capacity opera house for Broadway musicals; two cabaret theaters with a combined seating capacity of 1500; two virtual reality theaters; and a 300-room hotel. The design of each venue recalls Temecula's history as a former stagecoach and pony express stop. All structures and amenities are linked through Western themes and Old-West-style architecture.

Old Town's architecture is characterized by wood siding, shutters, one- and two-story massing, rectangular facades, balconies with balustrades, and exterior wood stairways. Design motifs are typical of designs introduced to Temecula in the 1880-1910 period. Streetscapes, standard utility poles, fire hydrants, drinking fountains, newspaper stands, and phone booths have been replaced with period-style fixtures.

Entertainment structures that enlivened the era — circus tents, Delta steamboats, and opera houses — have also been brought back to life. The Wild West arena, with its fabric top and removable sides, is a replica of the touring tent used by Buffalo Bill.

OLD TOWN TEMECULA ENTERTAINMENT CENTER

LOCATION
*Temecula, California
USA*

CLIENT
*The City of Temecula and
The Zev Buffman Group*

SITE SIZE
60 acres

PROJECT SIZE
650,000 square feet

AMENITIES
*4,800-seat Wild West arena;
2 hotels totaling 750 rooms;
opera house;
600-seat showboat theater;
100,000 square feet of
retail commercial space*

A *4,800-seat tent patterned after Buffalo Bill's touring show tents is designed to add color and to relate indoor and outdoor attractions.*

Each of the primary facilities, which include a 2,200-seat opera house and virtual reality pavilions, is themed to recall the particular history of Temecula, echoing a traditional Western-style architecture. The design blends larger-than-life period detailing with modern technology.

Architectural styles used in the Old Town Entertainment Center are typical of designs introduced to Temecula in the 1880-1910 period.

THE LOST CITY

Every part of the Lost City theme park was designed to depict a mythical story. In this way, the myth became a framework from which the design team could master-plan the overall effect of its evolution, appearance, each minute detail, and its execution and function.

The legend tells of a great earthquake that changed the course of rivers and created underground caverns, waterfalls, geysers, and other incredible phenomena that might still erupt without warning.

To make the legend seem real, The Lost City includes the largest combination of grand-scale water features found anywhere on earth. Among them are the world's largest man-made waterfall and lake with mechanically created, two-meter high surf.

To further depict the results of the catastrophic earthquake, the architects designed columns that stand askew and walkways that are split by cracks. Artificial ruins have been given an aged patina so that they appear to be thousands of years old. Newly-created bridges are made from aged, pre-stressed concrete. Structural detail work

appears rendered by ancient tools and processes to complete the fantasy. The gates of two mining entrances are made of hard-wrought iron attached with ancient methods of smelting; hinges are hammer-wrought. Window frames are hewn stone, and no wood frames or glass are used in The Lost City; all windows are open, with hand-carved wood grills.

The highest level of technology used on the project was employed in making the Bridge of Time. The bridge floats on rollers and required seismic design, motion initiators, and a streamlined hydraulic system, to mechanically simulate the shakes and rumbles of a 4-point earthquake every hour.

The designs of the new golf clubhouse, entertainment center, and extension to the casino follow The Lost City theme; even the arid 64-acre valley site was transformed into a man-made tropical jungle with over 1.6 million trees, plants, and shrubs.

The Lost City was completed in a record time of under three years. During that period, an entire domain was created, and a realm that had never really existed began to seem real even to its inventors.

LOCATION
*Republic of Bophuthatswana
South Africa
(100 miles northwest
of Johannesburg)*

CLIENT
*Sol Kerzner, Chairman,
Sun International, Ltd.*

SITE SIZE
68 acres

AMENITIES
*Water adventure park;
17 acres of lakes,
rivers, and jungles;
two 18-hole Gary Player
golf courses and other
recreational facilities;
golf clubhouse; casino gaming*

The Lost City golf course offers magnificent views and unique challenges, including live crocodiles as a permanent hazard on the 13th hole.

The sacred leopard on the Temple of Creation was devised from steel armature with precast and hand-built elements, all made on site. This structure is designed to conceal a portion of a preexisting casino built with warehouse construction.

*The golf clubhouse of
The Lost City utilizes
natural rock formations
of the region combined
with architectural
forms of early natives,
including designs based
on the mysterious
Zimbabwe Towers.*

*The ancient ruins
theme is carried into
the clubhouse interiors.
Columns and walls
were processed on-site
from sculpted cement
plaster over a masonry
core, then stressed and
strained for an aged
effect.*

*The Lost City includes
the largest combination
of grand-scale water
features found any-
where on earth. Inter-
connecting bodies of
water and extensive
plant life create a sense
of the tropics.*

*The Valley of Waves
includes 17 acres of
man-made rivers and
lakes offering guests the
choice of plunging
down near-vertical
water chutes, bobbing
in inflatable tubes, or
surfing a six-foot wave.*

PALM HILLS GOLF RESORT AND SPA

LOCATION
Okinawa, Japan

CLIENT
Takakura Corporation

SITE SIZE
12 acres

PROJECT SIZE
*135,000 square feet of golf
and spa facilities;
18-hole Ronald Fream/
Golfplan Design Group
championship course*

AMENITIES
*70-foot-high atrium with
grand stair; four restaurants;
VIP lounge; locker rooms
and baths of both
Japanese and Western style;
notable art collection;
interior and exterior gardens
and water features*

THE CLIENT AND THE ARCHITECT, meeting for the first time, were on an Okinawan hillside overlooking Itoman City and the sea beyond. They were viewing the site for a signature golf clubhouse and spa, the initial project for a new resort and cultural center. With typical American directness, the architect asked about the design objectives. The client had his own critical path. "Before we talk about design," he said, "I will take you to play golf with me. I want you to experience the Japanese way of playing golf."

Thus, the architect's second meeting with the client was a day devoted to golf, in Japanese translation. He learned that to play golf in Japan is to give oneself 100 percent to the entire procedure, savoring each element of the whole, which is conducted in measured stages, with prescribed, almost ritualistic, routine.

In subsequent meetings — all in good time — the architect learned that the client wanted a Mediterranean-style clubhouse and spa that would have a strong garden orientation and an elaborate suite for the exclusive use of the owner, whose personal art collection would be exhibited throughout the facility.

Armed with these facts and first-hand experience with the process of golf in Japan, the architect — working in concert with landscape architect and interior designer — was able to translate the client's mandate into a strikingly impressive Mediterranean-inspired architecture that also functions to accommodate uniquely Japanese conventions. On the course, for instance, ritual dictates a rest and something to eat and to drink at two halfway houses. Courtesy demands that caddies (uniformed women knowledgeable about golf and schooled in service) be brought a drink when players drink.

With complete and elaborate spa facilities, as well as four separate restaurants, the program for the clubhouse respects the rituals which follow a day of golf. At the conclusion of 18 holes of play, a steeped-in-tradition Japanese bath, in which scrub-down is preliminary to a communal hot soak, is *de rigueur*. Next, a bracing, cold plunge; meticulous grooming; and return to street clothes. Finally, a graciously presented dinner completes the day.

A showplace that embraces Western design and, at the same time spotlights Japanese cultural traditions, the Palm Hills Clubhouse and Spa sets the pace for subsequent elements of the Palm Hills resort.

In deference to Okinawa's cyclone susceptibility, finials atop a large atrium hold lightening rods, an anchorage system around glass areas supports protective panels used during threatening weather, and each roof tile is mortar-set. Broken roof forms give the building a residential scale.

The roof soars high above the Atrium Terrace, creating the opportunity for a garden-themed mezzanine level. The roof framework features a series of steel-enclosed, boxed-in trusses above stepped, recessed coffers around the ceiling perimeter. Decorative grillwork below functions as a vent.

In the elaborate VIP lounge, which offers private dining, the design theme is expressed in arches and French doors, windows with stepped relief, and small, subtle downlights that make key areas appear to be lit by chandeliers and table lamps.

As the initial project for an ambitious golf resort, Palm Hills embodies the owner's mandate for an impressive Mediterranean-inspired architecture that accommodates uniquely Japanese conventions. The men's furo (soaking bath) combines an opulent rendition of Japanese bathing customs and Western innovation.

IN THE HEART OF WEST Hollywood on the Sunset Strip, the client wanted to build a large-scale thematic interpretation of a Mississippi roadhouse of the early 1900s. This nightclub/restaurant/museum would celebrate an original American musical form — the blues — and revitalize the worldwide image of Hollywood as the entertainment capital of America. The

HOUSE OF BLUES

House of Blues was to be the most compelling, innovative music hall on the West Coast.

The architects designed the House of Blues in the style of an old-time, Southern juke-joint, exaggerated in form, evocative in atmosphere. Authentic materials of a bygone place and time have immediate impact; the exterior siding is corrugated tin that was brought in from Mississippi. Double-long windows flanked by narrow shutters recall the old shotgun houses of the rural South. Even in the eclectic, sophisticated mix of architectural styles along the strip, this scaled-up version of a roadhouse stands out and excites the imagination.

Inside, wood floors and beaded-board walls recreate the sepia world of the 1920s,

'30s, and '40s Mississippi Delta country from which the blues emerged. The architecture is purposely unrefined and provocative. Since the House of Blues was intended to offer serendipity in performance artists — major stars, new voices on the blues scene, and Sunday gospel sings are all part of the format — the design had to be versatile. The owners also wanted the flexibility of contracting or expanding public spaces depending on crowd size.

The ground-level nightclub has seating for 500, a large dance floor, and a stage, but can easily be sectioned off to create smaller venues. On the second level, an immense bar swings open like gigantic hinged doors to create a space through which guests can view the entertainment area below. On the uppermost level is a VIP lounge for special occasions, office spaces, and a retail outlet. This level opens to a terrace with a view of the Los Angeles Basin.

The House of Blues was built to glorify the Delta blues and its resurgence. Today, in this rustic structure, the origins of the music have been revived stylistically so that the blues tradition can live on.

LOCATION
West Hollywood, California
USA

CLIENT
Isaac Tigrett

SITE SIZE
2 acres

PROJECT SIZE
26,000 square feet;
1,000-person capacity;
3 levels

AMENITIES
250-seat restaurant;
50-foot bar; retail shop;
VIP lounge

The House of Blues, a combination restaurant and cultural center which celebrates the Delta blues, is conceived as an evocative, thematic rendition of a Mississippi roadhouse. Authentic materials — weathered siding, tin roofing, and beadedboard walls — recall another place and time.

The 500-person capacity night club, which includes dance floor and stage, is entered from the ground level. On the second level, the 250-seat restaurant can be divided for intimate seating or expanded onto a dining terrace overlooking downtown Los Angeles.

Flexibility is built into the design to allow contraction or expansion of restaurants, bars, stage, and dance floor depending on the occasion. The main restaurant's hinged, mechanized bar folds to allow viewing of stage and entertainment areas below.

137

In 1983, WHILE ATTENDING the grand opening of the newest tower at the Hilton Hawaiian Village, hotel magnate Barron Hilton surveyed the hodgepodge of buildings on the property from the tower's 35th floor and said, "There's more work to be done."

The hotel's master plan was born. The objectives: create order out of chaos;

HILTON HAWAIIAN VILLAGE

increase the open space; offer arriving guests a view of Hawaii's turquoise waters; and generally renovate, upgrade, and reposition the entire resort.

Through a four-phase schedule that lessened the amount of upheaval at any one time, the project was accomplished without major interruption to hotel operations. The work included demolition of several buildings; gutting and rebuilding one tower; renovation of old structures; design and construction of new structures; relocating and upgrading food and beverage outlets and many retail shops.

The redesign creates a special arrival experience with a dramatic new porte cochere and open-air reception pavilion offering ocean views and increased access to the beach. The resort's many functions — retail, convention, recreation, entertainment, and hospitality — are connected by creative landscaping which, in turn, plays a central role in developing a festive village atmosphere. Functionally, plantings provide visual screening, wind screening, and shade to protect against direct sunlight and to reduce ground temperature. Aesthetically, the landscape unifies the character of the village and gives each area its own identity.

A host of other design elements help create the feeling of a pleasurable tropical paradise: the curved line of spaces and walkways; the sensuousness of water (as expressed in pools, waterfalls, streams, ponds, gurgling jets, and the ocean itself); the flow of plants into interiors; changes in elevation; variety of texture; patterns in light and shade; and splashes of botanical color. The result: a rejuvenated resort, a village oasis in the heart of urban Waikiki.

LOCATION
Waikiki Beach – Honolulu
Oahu, Hawaii
USA

CLIENT
Hilton Hawaiian Village
Joint Venture (Hilton Hotels
Corporation and Prudential
Insurance Company of America)

SITE SIZE
20 oceanfront acres

PROJECT SIZE
A village of mixed-use buildings
2,523 hotel rooms

AMENITIES
10 restaurants and lounges;
100 specialty shops;
113,000 square feet of banquet
and conference space;
cabaret theatre; lagoon;
4 swimming pools; health club;
2 luau gardens

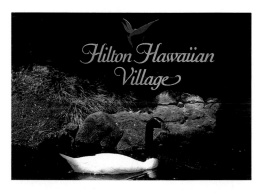

Created from semi-basement space, the new Rainbow Lanai coffee shop has two-story doors that open to individual dining pods overlooking a carp pool.

Through a four-phase schedule, the project was completed with minimal interruption to guests. During construction, the tropical paradise continued to provide a secluded beachfront oasis in the heart of urban Waikiki.

An outstanding example of contemporary Hawaiian architecture, the Hilton's open pavilions overlook a progression of water views: a pool with spurting water-jets; a 10,000-square-foot free-form swimming pool; and, beyond, a panoramic view of the Pacific Ocean.

With openness as the design goal, the architect helped the aging 20-acre Hilton Hawaiian Village attract a new market by demolishing some buildings; renovating others; building new ones; consolidating open spaces; relocating food/beverage/retail outlets; and adding major water features and extensive landscaping.

AVIARA GOLF CLUBHOUSE & ACADEMY

The Aviara Golf Clubhouse & Academy is the first element of a 1,100-acre, master-planned resort and residential community which will include a five-star, 350-room hotel with sport and tennis center. A primary goal was to achieve a high quality design for the 30,000 square foot facility which would set the tone architecturally for the luxury hotel and other residential developments to follow.

The design team chose Mission-style architecture as appropriate for the Southern California setting. Clay tile roofs; thick plaster walls with an evenly textured, troweled appearance; exposed wooden eaves; and wood doors and windows give character to the exteriors.

The site, one of Southern California's few remaining undeveloped ocean-view locations, was adjacent to a protected lagoon and had extensive environmental restrictions. After a review and approval process, height and width limitations were set; strong concerns were expressed by the city of Carlsbad and by area residents about possible changes in existing views.

Building into the sloping hillside site was one solution. This presents a one-story, low-key building from the street and along view corridors from neighboring homes. This approach also met height restrictions — 28 feet at midpoint of the clubhouse roof — and reduced impact on the surrounding environment.

A strong base element to the clubhouse building, as well as an extensive arcade on the southern exposure's lower level, creates interesting patterns of light and shadow while reducing perception of scale. Rooflines were kept simple. Extensive landscaping and land berms screen the clubhouse and academy from vehicular traffic and parking so that guests can enjoy a natural, unblemished setting.

The creation and preservation of views from within the clubhouse was another primary concern. All public areas have commanding views of Batiquitos Lagoon, a rich habitat for wetland plants and birds. The sitting room overlooks the first tee; the dining area overlooks the 18th fairway. Terraces circling the south elevation offer guests extensive views and the chance to enjoy the Southern California climate.

For residents and vacationers who enjoy the Aviara Golf Clubhouse & Academy, the restrictions on its design were turned into advantages. The Clubhouse is a major, world-class amenity for the entire Aviara development, for the city of Carlsbad, and for all of Southern California.

LOCATION
Carlsbad, California
USA

CLIENT
Aviara Resort Association

SITE SIZE
27.5 acres

PROJECT SIZE
33,500 square feet

AMENITIES
Pro shop; golf academy; administrative offices; 10,000-square-foot maintenance facility and comfort stations; Arnold Palmer-designed 18-hole golf course; driving range

Complementing the architectural style of the clubhouse, the information center houses administrative and marketing offices for the masterplanned resort.

By building into the site, the architects created an unimposing structure, met height limitations, and protected views of the lagoon for nearby residents.

Public spaces on the club-house's upper entry level, including a 2,000-square-foot dining room, lobby area and bar, can be opened to create multi-function areas for large gatherings.

The 33,500-square-foot Clubhouse and Academy is designed to set the architectural standard for an 1100-acre resort development to follow. To meet extensive environmental impact limitations of the coastal lagoon setting, the clubhouse is built into the hillside location.

1. CLUBHOUSE
2. ENTRY DRIVE
3. PARKING
4. SERVICE YARD
5. 18TH GREEN
6. LAKE
7. PUTTING GREEN
8. 1ST TEE
9. DRIVING RANGE

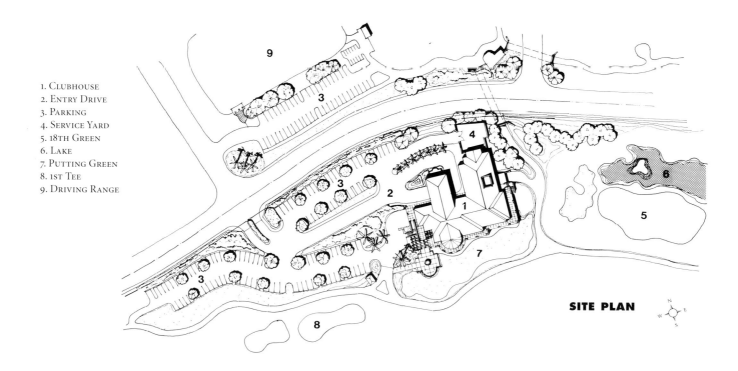

SITE PLAN

145

CHILDREN COME FIRST. That has always been the operating philosophy of the Danish toy-making giant. LEGO World Family Theme Park, located in Windsor, England, is designed to stimulate children's imagination and creativity and to encourage children to explore, experience, and express their own world.

LEGO WORLD FAMILY THEME PARK

As architect and lead consultant, WAT&G worked closely with a team that included the client, attraction specialists, landscape architects, engineers, and transportation planning experts, to develop a design for which no prototype existed. The LEGO Group knew they wanted children to be the focal point of the park, with elements that would encourage family interaction and learning, fun and creativity; but the specific content and theme of the park evolved during the initial design phases of the project.

The Windsor site, with its old oak trees and wonderful views, is itself a part of the experience. Activity clusters are surrounded by acres of woods and open parkland, making LEGO World a park within a park.

The park is comprised of six distinct clusters. The first one, The Beginning, is the main entry and welcome point for visitors to the theme park. The Hub is a cluster where guests can interact with LEGO products in their many forms. In Miniland, LEGO models depict famous buildings from various countries; and The Willows features DUPLO gardens, a puppet theater, and a boat ride for young children. Older kids enjoy My Town and Wild Woods — the latter features an enchanted forest and an adventure playground.

WAT&G designed low-rise, user-friendly buildings as an extension of the landscape. Careful attention was paid to the integration of hardscaping and landscaping to seamlessly blend the building entries and walkways with their surroundings.

While eager to create an environment that showcases its products, the client was sensitive about over using LEGO building blocks in the architectural imagery. On buildings where a LEGO-like quality was desired, extensive research was done to find cladding materials that would resemble over-sized LEGO elements but would not have to be made of plastic.

The buildings are of simple construction, with load-bearing masonry walls, steel columns, and metal truss roof structures. The exterior finishes consist mostly of plaster with applied graphics and color.

Throughout the project, every attempt was made to use standard detailing and construction to maintain quality and to manage costs. Without the typical white-knuckle rides, LEGO World Family Theme Park excites its visitors with walk-through experiences and opportunities for creative play, proving that entertainment and education can mix together splendidly.

LOCATION
Windsor, England

CLIENT
LEGO World A/S

SITE SIZE
177 acres

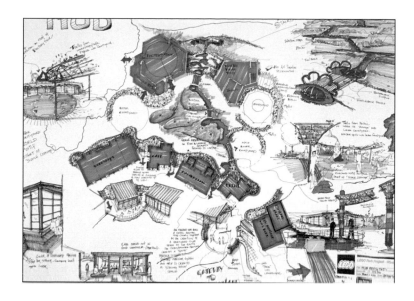

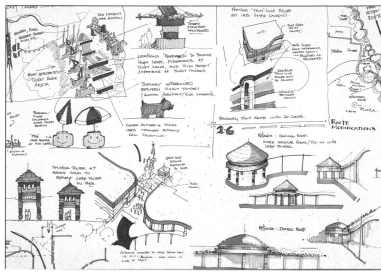

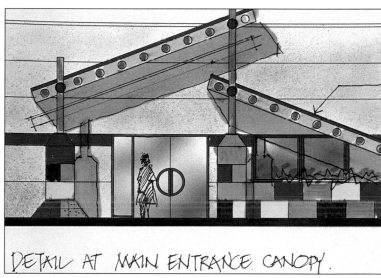

DETAIL AT MAIN ENTRANCE CANOPY.

A SPA, A MEDICAL FACILITY, a salon, a golf resort, a corporate training facility, a hotel, a conference center, a creative arts studio, a smorgasbord of restaurants, a recreational paradise with nine tennis courts and eight swimming pools: all of these dissimilar diversions are gracefully combined at the Hyatt Regency Coolum.

Australia's first international health management residential resort is appropriately set among 370 acres (150 hectares) of lush rainforest and bushland, fronting almost a mile of Pacific Ocean beach. This project, with a village-plan concept, is designed to provide both rest and stimulation.

In an effort to give the resort complex a residential feeling, everything is decentralized. Instead of a central lobby, there is a village square where guests can eat, shop,

HYATT REGENCY COOLUM INTERNATIONAL RESORT & SPA

drink, and be entertained. Guest quarters, too, are grouped in three low-rise clusters set amongst the trees.

All of the 330 units are located around nine individual guest lounges, where guests can gather for breakfast and a variety of informal social activities throughout the day. The spaces between the clusters are as important as the buildings themselves. Pathways link all aspects of the resort, and guests are encouraged to walk or bike along these "corridors."

The architecture is inspired by elements of the Queensland style: lattices, trellises, and louvres provide shade and create interesting patterns and textures. Similarly, colors are borrowed from those seen in Coolum's rainforests, mountains, coastal marshes, and beaches.

Based on the belief that maximum performance in the business arena needs to be balanced with physical well-being, the resort offers an opportunity to do both — and optimize each.

LOCATION
Coolum Beach
Queensland, Australia

CLIENT
Kumagi Guam Pty. Ltd.

SITE SIZE
370 acres

PROJECT SIZE
330 units
(174 villas and 156 suites)

AMENITIES
9 tennis courts; Robert Trent Jones II championship golf course; 8 swimming pools; spa, salon; health management center; conference facilities; beach club; squash courts; creative arts center

Set amidst rainforest and bushland, and bordered by Mt. Coolum and the Pacific Ocean, the project was conceived as a health management resort village.

Guests arrive at the dramatic port cochere leading to the reception building, which houses restaurants and lounges and serves as the resort's golf clubhouse, as well.

A bold contemporary version of Queensland-inspired architecture. Petrie's restaurant incorporates time-honored shading devices and the familiar post-modern lines of a corrugated metal roof.

In keeping with the health-oriented design plan, a town square replaces the traditional hotel lobby, and accommodations are spread out to encourage guests to walk or ride bicycles.

Built on a decentralized village plan, Hyatt Regency Coolum's restaurants are served by a single commissary with a containerized supply and waste disposal system.

Queensland's vernacular architecture is a good fit for modestly budgeted design programs aimed at an upscale market. A generous use of exposed indigenous woods in one- and two-story stucco buildings eliminates glitz in favor of simple, climate-wise cottages.

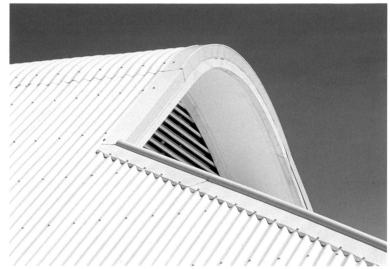

MEMBERS AND GUESTS WHO spend time at the Wailea Golf Clubhouse recognize that it is more than just a pretty place. Designed to service two golf courses, the clubhouse must function at full efficiency for golfers and also meet the social requirements inherent in such a multi-purpose building type.

The clubhouse was designed to create a comfortable, Hawaiian-estate atmosphere by

WAILEA GOLF CLUBHOUSE

incorporating a generous lobby with atrium, porte cochere for bag drop-off, serene water features, a spacious pro shop, restaurant, dining terraces, and private lounges.

The sequential placement of cart drop-off, pick-up, and cart path assures an efficient traffic pattern greatly appreciated by golfers.

The non-golfing, social side of golf has come to have its own ideal conditions, and these include being able to keep your eyes on the ball from inside the clubhouse as well as while on the greens. The architect, therefore, positioned major public spaces at vantage points which provide spectators

with excellent views of action on the golf courses. Well-settled into the undulations of a gentle slope, the Wailea Golf Clubhouse spreads across a wide expanse of manicured green overlooking panoramic views of fairways, ocean, and two distant, offshore islands. The major view-sited spaces face significant holes: the first, ninth, tenth, and eighteenth. For visual control, the starter's box also shares this choice viewpoint.

With its massive, grey-green ceramic tile roof and sheltering eaves, French doors and tall casement windows, cut limestone columns and stucco exterior, this sprawling structure evokes memories of the climate- and culture-sensitive Hawaiian architecture that evolved and flourished in the 1920s and 1930s. Generous overhangs provide shade, and the open-air design takes advantage of prevailing trade winds. Pergolas and broad, stepped terraces link the indoors to outdoors, taking advantage of southern Maui's sunny climate. Extensive use of decorative grillwork seals the project's identity as Hawaiian classic, a comfortable, refined response to a tropical community of diverse cultures.

LOCATION
Wailea, Maui, Hawaii
USA

CLIENT
Wailea Resort Company, Ltd.

SITE SIZE
337 acres

PROJECT SIZE
60,030 square feet

AMENITIES
Two 18-hole Robert Trent Jones II golf courses; one 18-hole Jack Snyder course; lobby with 38-foot skylight; two reflecting pools; storage for 800 bags; parking for 350; underground barn for 200 golf carts; interior landscaping; extensive terracing

Wailea Golf Clubhouse seems to hug the rolling terrain as the structure sprawls beneath the wide overhangs of a double-pitched, ceramic-tile roof. Terraces and vine-covered pergolas blur indoor-outdoor boundaries as they create uniquely "Hawaiian" living space.

The clubhouse restaurant offers more than 9,500 square feet of dining space, about half of which is on terraces that take full advantage of panoramic views of the course, the ocean, and offshore islands.

A large full-service pro shop with extensive retail space shares the main level with a porte cochere, entryway, lobby, formal lounges, restaurant, kitchen, starter-box, bag-rental shop, offices, and locker rooms. Carts, service, and storage areas are nestled unobtrusively under a slope on the lower level.

TANJONG JARA BEACH HOTEL/RANTAU ABANG VISITOR CENTER

LOCATION
Kuala, Terengganu
Malaysia

CLIENT
Malaysian Government Tourism
Development Council

SITE SIZE
76 acres, Tanjong Jara;
15 acres, Rantau Abang

PROJECT SIZE
97,595 square feet,
100 cottage rooms, Tanjong Jara;
21,434 square feet,
10 chalets, Rantau Abang

AMENITIES
Tanjong Jara – swimming pool;
swimming lagoon; game rooms;
tennis and squash courts; spa.
Rantau Abang – sea life museum;
turtle-watching observation deck;
handicraft bazaar

WHEN A FIRM ACHIEVES international acclaim for one of its most modest, low-budget, leisure-oriented projects by winning the coveted Aga Khan Award for Architecture, what does that project say about the firm?

In the case of WAT&G, Tanjong Jara Beach Hotel, and its companion project, Rantau Abang Visitor Center, both say the architects valued the small job as highly as any large commission. Staff made numerous trips to Malaysia to research the historic architecture of the area, the Malaysian culture and climate, history and art, geography, economics, raw materials, and religion. They learned enough about East Coast Malaysia, its people, and their heritage of land and sea to design a project imbued with the very essence of its locale and one that has an added dimension, a sense of place that makes it Malaysia in microcosm.

The basic design motif for the buildings of Tanjong Jara and Rantau Abang was found in the indigenous and consummately leisure-oriented *istanas*, the elegantly crafted wooden palaces of Malaysian sultans of long ago. Climate-wise and cost-effective to build, they were also readily adaptable to contemporary hotel requirements. The building form, which evolved over centuries, is eminently practical in relationship to local weather conditions; it makes use of materials plentiful in the area and features traditional Malaysian art forms and craftsmanship. The one- and two-story hardwood buildings are constructed three to five feet above the ground for purposes of security, flood protection, and air circulation.

Other ventilating devices that respond to the humid, tropical climate are open-sided rooms, lattice soffits, multiple-pitch roofs and gable grilles, and locally made bisque roof tiles left exposed on the inside, allowing the warm air to escape through the roof.

Native hardwood, milled on site and allowed to weather naturally, is used in all building construction. Decorative motifs employ authentic Malaysian arts and crafts, including wood carvings, woven mats, baskets, kites, and ceramics, and make them an integral part of the design.

The Aga Khan Award jurors cited Tanjong Jara and Rantau Abang for the courage to search out and successfully adapt and develop an otherwise rapidly disappearing traditional architecture and craft, to meet the demands of contemporary architecture.

As local hardwoods are abundant in the area, native craftsmen relearned traditional building skills to construct the resort almost exclusively of native woods.

No taller than a coconut tree, Tanjong Jara Beach Hotel celebrates the Malaysian vernacular with a style patterned after the wooden palaces of long-ago sultans.

Concrete was the only modern material employed in construction of the hotel. Its use was limited to the footings and as a thin slab placed between floors to suppress noise.

WEST ELEVATION

1. MUSEUM
2. COCKTAIL BAR
3. SNACK SHOP
4. SHOPS
5. SHELTERED LANDINGS
6. BAZAAR
7. ENTRANCE DRIVE

Rooftops of locally made bisque tile cover the buildings in the complex. The underside of the tile is left exposed on the interior, allowing air to circulate in guest rooms and warm air to escape through the roof.

Rantau Abang Visitor Center houses a turtle museum. Built on stilts above the water to lessen the likelihood of human interference with turtles' annual egg-laying ritual, the museum's deck also functions as a turtle viewing platform.

SITE SECTION

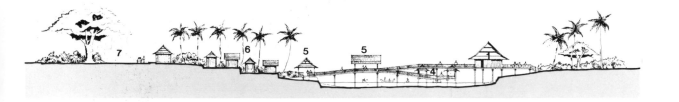

THAT FUTURE WITH A FUNNY NAME

A Prediction by Ray Bradbury

HOW DO YOU SPELL THE FUTURE TO MAKE SURE IT HAPPENS IN THE RIGHT WAY?

It has always seemed to me that while the politicians are hoisting themselves up in their hot-air balloons with no ballast, going nowhere, you run along ahead of them and — invent the future. Build it while no one is looking. Dream the cliché-impossible-dream that everyone doubts and no one believes in until they wind up next door to or surrounded by it and, too late, they're in love.

I have seen the future and it is more than a promised land and we don't have to march there, it is near at hand; its roots are in Hawaii and its gardens are across the world. It is a future with a funny name: *Wimberly Allison Tong & Goo.*

No, this is not a postcard I'm writing and sending from Hyperbole, Kansas.

How did I come to the uncomfortable position of spokesperson for this glorious view of tomorrow? Prepare yourself for coincidence.

I did some minor consulting work on the Orbitron ride at EuroDisney outside Paris, a few years ago. After attending the opening day ceremonies, I went up to the second floor of the Disneyland Hotel in the late afternoon to sit with a cold beer and a fine view of the new park, musing on its many qualities.

Halfway through my drink a stranger walked up and asked permission to sit at my table. I agreed, amiably, and we chatted for a few minutes about the park, the happy celebration, and that night's fireworks. I looked around at the hotel and praised it, saying it was very fine.

But, I added, *I know a hotel finer than this. The greatest, to me anyway, hotel in the world, and I've lived in dozens of them!*

What hotel is that? said the stranger.

The Grand Floridian, at Disney World, Florida, I said, working up steam.

Everything about it invites. The shape, the size, the colors, the restaurants. And the main lobby which rises at least six floors above the conversational area below, and gives kids notions about running up there to circle round and think about spitting down at their parents, below. What a place! The Grand Floridian. Go there!

I've been, said the stranger. *That's mine. Yours?*

Ours, I should say. Our architectural firm designed it.

My God, I cried. *And here I've been shooting off my mouth — !*

It's all right, said Jerry Allison, reaching out to shake my hand, laughing. *Don't stop.*

I haven't. I'm still saying the same, only more so. Since then, I've stayed again at the Grand Floridian and see no reason to change. I'd still like to run up to the sixth floor to sail paper planes or spit. I always leave there a foot shorter and ten times louder than when I came through the door.

Can these architects solve and improve everything? No. But they can slow Big-Brother in his tracks. They can nibble and nick and munch around the edges of time and, bit by bit, change cities that have fallen to skeleton and skin, give life to dying cultures, and wake up the ones that are just dormant.

Politics seem to have no cure for our empty boulevards and parks, but corporate cash and architectural imagination can guarantee at least safe walking and living places. Schweitzer once said, do something good, someone may imitate it. These architects can set examples near cities, if not in them, to be seen and imitated.

Wimberly Allison Tong & Goo, like Gaul, exists in four parts, but the four parts make a whole that can lick the jeesuz out of a small part of the future.

While a good part of Africa self-destroys, in Bophuthatswana inventors from Wimberly Allison Tong & Goo discover a civilization that never was, and promise a future not over the rainbow, but underfoot. I would go there, to their bee-loud glades.

So what follows are not postcards from the future. They are good promises that can and will be kept. Big Brother will never be dead. But they're giving him a rough time.

PALM BEACH RESORT HOTEL & CASINO
Cannes, France

RECALLING THE MAGICAL EPOCH of the grand hotel, the Palm Beach Resort Hotel & Casino derives from historic influences found within the city of Cannes and the surrounding Riviera. The buildings are capped with low-pitched, tile roofs and arranged around classic garden courtyards designed to accommodate a variety of events.

EL MORRO PUNTA IXTAPA
Ixtapa, Mexico

THE HEART OF A MASTER-PLANNED resort community, El Morro Punta Ixtapa consists of 33 spacious condominium units in four buildings with two beach clubs, a retail center, chapel, pro shop pavilion with tennis and racquetball courts, and a maintenance/service center. The design is adapted from the traditional Palapa-style architecture of Mexico's Pacific Coast.

Dan Nichol

PETRA RESORT
Jordan

WITH ITS PETROGLYPHS and rock house temples, Petra is an international tourist destination. The hotel is designed as a hillside village, spread across three terraced levels and incorporating a panoramic mountain view. A variety of balconies, pergolas, window heights, and roof treatments give the buildings a Middle-Eastern quality, and traditional construction methods do the same. A partially-restored, ancient tower on the site is featured in the hotel's village square.

John Kingsley-Dobson

ABJAR HOTEL & BEACH CLUB
Dubai, United Arab Emirates

OVERLOOKING 1,000 FEET of the Gulf Coast, this is the first beachfront resort hotel in Dubai. Indigenous design elements and detailing taken from traditional Arabic decor are skillfully blended with the Berber-inspired Mediterranean vernacular to give the project a sense of regionalism and timelessness. One hundred and fifty rooms and extensive club facilities are developed as phase one; a conference center and additional 350-room tower will complete phase two.

John Kingsley-Dobson

164

DEAD SEA RESORT
Jordan

SITUATED ON THE EARTH's lowest point, this unique resort is designed to meet the recuperative and recreational needs of its visitors. The resort village echoes indigenous building forms and shade structures, and is heavily landscaped with water features throughout. A main pedestrian route, modeled after a cobblestone street in Jerusalem, leads from the lobby to the sea.

John Engsley-Dobson

KEWALO MARITIME VILLAGE
Honolulu, Hawaii

PATTERNED AS A TROPICAL seaside town, this mixed use nine acre site brings retail, offices, and entertainment to a vibrant and historic small-boat harbor in the center of a city. A variety of public spaces and a diversity of architectural styles reflect and reinforce the multicultural community of Honolulu.

Charlie Giles

DAECHIDONG
Seoul, Korea

DAECHIDONG IS A MIXED-USE building that vertically stacks five parking levels and two retail levels below grade. Ten floors of retail space, four of office space, and six containing a sports center, meeting facilities, and roof-top restaurant are above grade. The ten retail levels above grade are visually linked by a transparent facade enclosing the atrium space.

Jose Alano

OAK VALLEY RESORT
Kang-Won-Do, Korea

FOUR THOUSAND RURAL ACRES provide a scenic backdrop to this complete destination resort. Patterned as a hillside village, Oak Valley Resort is surrounded by a 27-hole Robert Trent Jones II golf course and includes a five-star hotel, time-share condominiums, single-family residences, retail shops, a fitness center, an art gallery, a private-membership golf clubhouse, and even a wedding chapel.

Dauser & Kim

LEELA PALACE
Bombay, India

WITH SLENDER COLUMNS and intricately detailed arches, this 10-story, 275-room hotel feels both palatial and residential. Copper-clad, pyramid-shaped roofs and skyward-reaching towers are set against richly appointed atria, contributing to the elegance and regionality of this building.

Hausher & Kim

167

MONTERREY HOTEL
Monterrey, Mexico

THE 27-STORY, 729-ROOM Monterrey Hotel resembles an urban sculpture set on a four-story podium of stone; the sleek glass-and-metal tower reflects the changes of the sun and is curved to match the form of the site. The hotel's luxurious rooms, two restaurants, gymnasium, discotheque, retail shops, and meeting facilities augment Monterrey's newly-completed convention center across the street.

Barry Zauss

JURONG LAKE
Singapore

THIS MULTI-FACETED DEVELOPMENT, with entertainment and recreation complex, theme park, resort, commercial center, and park system, is conceived as a new destination for both Singaporeans and international visitors. Imagery for the Jurong Lake development takes its inspiration from the Jurong Dragon, whose legend was created by the architects.

Anthony Van Strauhal/Bob Eding

BALI NIRWANA RESORT
Tabanan, Bali, Indonesia

BEYOND A WIDE CRESCENT of sand on Bali's south coast is the 299-acre Bali Nirwana Resort. The site features the five-star Le Meridien Hotel with seaside amphitheater, sports center, and club-house, and a 30,000-square-foot thalassotherapy spa. Integrated into the resort are over 700 residential units, including 380 resort homes, 160 luxury villas, and 150 timeshare units.

ADM

PLAZA HOTEL KEMPINSKI
Jakarta, Indonesia

LOCATED ON A 3.5-ACRE SITE in the central business district of Jakarta, this streamlined tower contains a 350-room hotel, along with 260 luxury condominium residences on its upper floors. The overall concept is of an urban retreat with gardens, business center, pool terrace, fitness center, and a traditional German beerhouse.

Barry Zauss

PALAU HILTON RESORT
Palau

THIS 200-ROOM RESORT is set among 25 acres of lush tropical forest, on a sloping site that allows for ocean views in every guest room and public space. Gardens and streams connect all of the resort's elements: restaurants, retail shops, a health club, conference rooms, swimming pools, and a Palauan craft village.

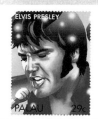

Hausher & Kim

MERCHANT ROAD HOTEL
Singapore

CAPTURING THE SPIRIT and heritage of cosmopolitan Singapore, this 381-room hotel capitalizes on its prime waterfront setting. Surrounding the building at ground level, an active colonnade draws the public in to enjoy the hotel's many restaurants, pubs, and shops. A roof-deck garden courtyard — with cascading pools, spa facilities, and lush tropical plants — opens up to a carefully framed view of the Singapore River.

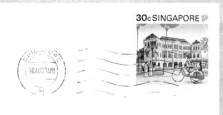

Hausher & Kim

171

KUNINGAN PERSADA
MIXED-USE DEVELOPMENT
Jakarta, Indonesia

THIS CONTEMPORARY MIXED-USE development is conceived as an international marketplace of themed microenvironments. Together, they constitute a mini-city with two retail complexes; a 32-story office tower; two entertainment centers; a 700-room hotel; a conference center; serviced apartment complex; and parking for 3,800 cars.

JOHOR BAHRU CITY HARBOUR MARINA

Johor Bahru, Malaysia

THE INTENT OF THIS three-marina, mixed-use project is to re-orient Johor Bahru to the sea. A vibrant mix of hotels, retail shops, offices, and condominiums are angled toward the marina and sea vistas. The marine identity is further reinforced with the presence of a maritime museum and a customs house.

Fisher & Kim

PHOENIX WORLD CITY

Home Base: Port Canaveral, Florida

THE PHOENIX IS A CITY AT SEA. The quarter-mile-long, $1 billion vessel — three times larger than any passenger ship yet built — will carry up to 6,200 passengers. Visitors will disembark from a 400-passenger shuttle craft and step into a self-contained world inside the Phoenix with shops, art galleries, a 2,000-seat theater, a museum, a 100,000-volume library, and a sports complex. Most staterooms will be located in three hotel towers, rising eight decks above the hull.

Courtesy of World City Corporation

CHRONOLOGY

The following projects represent a cross-section of the hundreds of hospitality and leisure projects designed by Wimberly Allison Tong & Goo in the last half century.

1946 *Royal Hawaiian Hotel (renovation)*

LOCATION: *Waikiki Beach, Honolulu, Hawaii*
CLIENT: *Matson Hotel Company*
ASSOCIATE ARCHITECT: *Gardner Dailey, San Francisco*

1954 *Canlis Restaurant*

LOCATION: *Waikiki, Honolulu, Hawaii*
CLIENT: *Peter Canlis*
ASSOCIATE ARCHITECT: *Terry & Moore, AIA*
CONTRACTOR: *Nordic Construction Co.*
LANDSCAPE: *John Dominis Holt*
INTERIOR DESIGN: *Terry & Moore, AIA*

1956 *Coco Palms*

LOCATION: *Wailua Beach, Lihue, Kauai, Hawaii*
CLIENT: *Island Holidays Resorts, An Amfac Company*
CONTRACTOR: *Guy Matsunaga*
INTERIOR DESIGN: *Grace Buscher Guslander*

The Waikikian Hotel

LOCATION: *Waikiki, Honolulu, Hawaii*
CLIENT: *Waikikian Corporation*
CONTRACTOR: *Hawaiian Dredging Company, Ltd.*
LANDSCAPE: *George Walters*
INTERIOR DESIGN: *Murph Dailey*
STRUCTURAL ENGINEERING: *Richard R. Bradshaw*

1958 *Hotel Tahiti*

LOCATION: *Papeete, Tahiti, French Polynesia*
CLIENT: *Spencecliff Corporation*

1961 *Hotel Bora Bora*

LOCATION: *Bora Bora, Tahiti, French Polynesia*
CLIENT: *Société de Hôtelière Tahara'a, J.H. Long & Co., Inc.*
ASSOCIATE ARCHITECT: *Michel Prevot, Tahiti*
CONTRACTOR: *Local labor under owner's representative, Ed Fearon*

1963   *Sheraton Maui*

LOCATION: *Kaanapali Beach Resort, Kaanapali, Maui, Hawaii*
CLIENT: *Sheraton Corporation*
CONTRACTOR: *Swinerton, Walberg, Westgate & Tait*
LANDSCAPE: *George Walters*
INTERIOR DESIGN: *Mary Kennedy/Sheraton Corporation*

1966   *Pago Pago Inter-Continental Hotel*

LOCATION: *Pago Pago, American Samoa*
CLIENT: *American Samoan Development Corporation*
CONTRACTOR: *Swinerton, Walberg & Westgate (original construction)*
   Fletcher Construction (1980 reconstruction)
LANDSCAPE: *George Walters*
INTERIOR DESIGN: *Neal A. Prince/Intercontinental Hotels*

1967   *Fijian Hotel*

LOCATION: *Yanuca Island, Fiji*
CLIENT: *Fiji Resorts, Ltd.*
ASSOCIATE ARCHITECT: *Architects Pacific Design Partnership, Suva, Fiji*
CONTRACTOR: *Yee & Morgan, Suva*
LANDSCAPE: *Belt Collins Hawaii*
INTERIOR DESIGN: *Phyllis Brownlee*

1968   *Mauna Kea Beach Hotel, South Wing*

LOCATION: *South Kohala Coast, Hawaii*
CLIENT: *Rockresorts, Inc. (Lawrence S. Rockefeller & Eastern Airlines)*
CONTRACTOR: *Hawaiian Dredging Construction*
LANDSCAPE: *Belt Collins Hawaii*
INTERIOR DESIGN: *Phyllis K. Brownlee/PK Interiors, Honolulu*

Mount Rainier Visitor Center

LOCATION: *Mount Rainier National Park, Washington*
CLIENT: *U.S. Dept. of Interior*
ASSOCIATE ARCHITECT: *McGuire & Muri, Tacoma, Washington*
CONTRACTOR: *Eazley Contruction Company*
LANDSCAPE: *U.S. National Park Service*
ENGINEERING: *Anderson, Birkeland, Anderson & Mast*

1969   *Hyatt Regency Tahara'a*

LOCATION: *Matarai Bay, Tahiti, French Polynesia*
CLIENT: *Societe Hoteliere de Tahara'a*
ASSOCIATE ARCHITECT: *Michel Prevot, Tahiti*
CONTRACTOR: *Swinerton & Walberg Co.*
INTERIOR DESIGN: *Neal A. Prince/InterContinental*

1971 Sheraton Waikiki

LOCATION: *Waikiki Beach, Honolulu, Hawaii*
CLIENT: *ITT Sheraton Corporation of America*
CONTRACTOR: *Swinerton & Walberg Co.*

1975 Hanalei Bay Resort

LOCATION: *Princeville, Hanalei, Maui, Hawaii*
CLIENT: *General Hawaiian Development Corporation*
CONTRACTOR: *Pacific Construction Co., Ltd.*
LANDSCAPE: *Belt Collins Hawaii*
INTERIOR DESIGN: *Richard Crowell Associates/Dora Kuo Interiors*

1976 Hyatt Regency Waikiki, Hemmeter Center

LOCATION: *Waikiki, Honolulu, Hawaii*
CLIENT: *Hemmeter Development Corporation*
ASSOCIATE ARCHITECT: *Lawton & Taylor, Honolulu*
CONTRACTOR: *Swinerton and Walberg Co.*
LANDSCAPE: *Belt Colllins Hawaii*
INTERIOR DESIGN: *Harry McCague Associates/Richard Crowell Associates*

1977 Colony Kaluakoi Hotel & Golf Club

LOCATION: *Maunaloa, Molokai, Hawaii*
CLIENT: *Kepuhi Partnership*
CONTRACTOR: *Pacific Construction Co., Goodfellow Bros., Inc.*
LANDSCAPE: *Iwamoto & Associates*
INTERIOR DESIGN: *Richard Crowell Associates*

1978 International Market Place/Banyan Bazaar

LOCATION: *Waikiki, Honolulu, Hawaii*
CLIENT: *Waikiki Development Co.*
CONTRACTOR: *Trousdale Construction Company*
LANDSCAPE: *Melvin Lau & Associates*
MARKET PLACE CONCEPT: *Donn Beach*

Shangri-La Hotel, Garden Wing

LOCATION: *Singapore*
CLIENT: *Shangri-La Hotel*
ASSOCIATE ARCHITECT: *Archiplan Team, Singapore*
CONTRACTOR: *Paul Y. Construction (S) Pte. Ltd.*
LANDSCAPE: *Belt Collins Hawaii*
INTERIOR DESIGN: *Western International Hotels*

1980 Hyatt Regency Maui

LOCATION: *Kaanapali Beach Resort, Lahaina, Maui, Hawaii*
CLIENT: *Hemmeter Maui Development Company*
ASSOCIATE ARCHITECT: *Lawton & Umemura, AIA*
CONTRACTOR: *Hawaiian Dredging Construction Company*
LANDSCAPE: *Tongg Associates, Inc.*
INTERIOR DESIGN: *Howard-Hirsch & Associates/Harry Stoff Interiors*

1981 Tanjong Jara Beach Hotel/Rantau Abang Visitor Center

LOCATION: *Terengganu, Malaysia*
CLIENT: *Malaysia Government Tourism Development Council*
ASSOCIATE ARCHITECT: *Akitek Bersekutu, Malaysia*
CONTRACTOR: *Chew-Piau Construction Sdn. Bhd.*
LANDSCAPE: *Belt Collins Hawaii*
INTERIOR DESIGN: *Juru Hiasan Consult Sdn. Bwd., Kuala Lumpur*

1983 Sheraton Auckland

LOCATION: *Auckland, New Zealand*
CLIENT: *Rob Tennent/Devon Development Ltd.*
ASSOCIATE ARCHITECT: *Beca Carter Hollings & Ferner, Ltd., Auckland*
CONTRACTOR: *Fletcher Construction*
INTERIOR DESIGN: *Bent Severin/Alan Gilbert & Associates*

Arcadia Condominiums

LOCATION: *Singapore*
CLIENT: *Arcadia Gardens Pte. Ltd.*
ASSOCIATE ARCHITECT: *Chua Ka Seng & Partners Chartered Architects*
CONTRACTOR: *Paul Y. Construction Pte. Ltd.*
LANDSCAPE: *BCP Far East Ltd.*
INTERIOR DESIGN: *Chhada Siembieda & Associates Pte. Ltd.*

The Regent of Bangkok

LOCATION: *Bangkok, Thailand*
CLIENT: *The Rajdamri Hotel Company*
ASSOCIATE ARCHITECT: *Dan Wongprasat, Bangkok*
CONTRACTOR: *Kay Thai Construction Ltd.*
LANDSCAPE: *Khun Sittiporn Donavanik*
INTERIOR DESIGN: *Rifenberg/Rirkrit*

Turtle Bay Hilton (renovation)

LOCATION: *Kahuku, Oahu, Hawaii*
CLIENT: *Prudential Insurance Company*
CONTRACTOR: *Albert C. Kobayashi*
INTERIOR DESIGN: *Richard Crowell Associates/Charles Heen & Associates*

1984 *Sheraton Brisbane Hotel and Towers*

LOCATION: *Brisbane, Queensland, Australia*
CLIENT: *State Government Insurance Office, Queensland*
ASSOCIATE ARCHITECT: *Conrad & Gargett Pty. Ltd.*
CONTRACTOR: *Civil & Civic Pty. Ltd.*
INTERIOR DESIGN: *Graham Solano Pty. Ltd.,*
  James Penny Interior Design Consultants

The Ritz-Carlton, Laguna Niguel

LOCATION: *Dana Point, California*
CLIENT: *W.B. Johnson Properties, Inc.*
CONTRACTOR: *Stolte Inc.*
LANDSCAPE: *Peridian Group*
INTERIOR DESIGN: *Frank Nicholson, Inc.*

1985 *The Ritz-Carlton, Naples*

LOCATION: *Naples, Florida*
CLIENT: *W.B. Johnson Properties, Inc.*
ASSOCIATE ARCHITECT: *Milton Pate Associates Inc.*
CONTRACTOR: *Metric Constructors*
LANDSCAPE: *Foster, Conant & Associates, Inc., Orlando, Florida*
INTERIOR DESIGN: *Frank Nicholson, Inc.*

Hyatt Regency Cheju

LOCATION: *Cheju Island, Korea*
CLIENT: *Namju Development Company*
ASSOCIATE ARCHITECT: *Seoung Bae Shin*
CONTRACTOR: *ICC Construction Co., Ltd.*
LANDSCAPE: *Tongg Clarke & Mechler/Seoin Design*
INTERIOR DESIGN: *Chhada Siembieda & Associates, Ltd.*

1986 *Four Seasons Hotel Newport Beach*

LOCATION: *Newport Beach, California*
CLIENT: *The Irvine Company*
CONTRACTOR: *Dinwiddlie Construction Company*
LANDSCAPE: *Peridian Group/SWA*
INTERIOR DESIGN: *James Northcutt Associates*

Pacific Islands Club Guam

LOCATION: *Tumon, Agana, Guam*
CLIENT: *Inter-Pacific Resorts*
ASSOCIATE ARCHITECT: *Taniguchi-Ruth-Smith & Associates, Guam*
CONTRACTOR: *Black Construction Co./Fletcher Pacific*
LANDSCAPE: *Belt Collins Hawaii*
INTERIOR DESIGN: *Richard Crowell Associates*

1986 *Ramada Great Barrier Reef Resort*

LOCATION: *Palm Cove Bay, Cairns, Australia*
CLIENT: *International Resort Pty. Australia*
ASSOCIATE ARCHITECT: *Stenders Wright & Partners Pty. Ltd.,*
   Urban Designers, Town Planners, Brisbane
CONTRACTOR: *Solander Industries Pty. Ltd.*
LANDSCAPE: *Siteplan*
INTERIOR DESIGN: *Chhada Siembieda & Associates*

1988 *Disney's© Grand Floridian Beach Resort*

LOCATION: *Walt Disney World, Lake Buena Vista, Florida*
CLIENT: *Disney Development Company*
CONTRACTOR: *Frank J. Rooney, Inc.*
LANDSCAPE: *Peridian Group*
INTERIOR DESIGN: *Intradesign*

Hilton Hawaiian Village

LOCATION: *Waikiki Beach, Honolulu, Hawaii*
CLIENT: *Hilton Hawaiian Village Joint Venture*
   (Hilton Hotels Corporation and Prudential Insurance Company of America)
CONTRACTOR: *Albert C. Kobayashi, Inc.*
LANDSCAPE: *Woolsey, Miyabara & Associated, Inc.*
INTERIOR DESIGN: *Hirsch-Bedner & Associates/Hilton Corporation Design Studio*

Hyatt Regency Bellevue

LOCATION: *Bellevue, Washington*
CLIENT: *Kemper Development Company*
ASSOCIATE ARCHITECT: *Kober, Selater & Associates, Seattle*
CONTRACTOR: *Baugh Construction Company*
LANDSCAPE: *Jongejan, Gerrard & McNeal, Inc.*
INTERIOR DESIGN: *Richard Mayhew/Intradesign, Inc.*
SPACE PLANNING: *Marvin Stein Associates*

Hyatt Regency Coolum International Resort & Spa

LOCATION: *Coolum Beach, Queensland, Australia*   OVERALL CONCEPT: *Dr. John Tickell*
CLIENT: *Kumugai Gumi Pty. Ltd.*   VILLAGE CONCEPT: *Bernd Chorengel*
   Concrete Construction Pty. Ltd.
ASSOCIATE ARCHITECT: *Bligh Robinson, Australia*
CONTRACTOR: *Concrete Construction Pty. Ltd.*
LANDSCAPE: *Tongg Clarke & Mechler*
INTERIOR DESIGN: *Hirsch-Bedner & Associates*

Parkroyal Shopping Village/Cairns International

LOCATION: *Cairns, Queensland, Australia*
CLIENT: *Hal McGowan*
ASSOCIATE ARCHITECT: *Clarke & Prince Pty. Ltd.*
CONTRACTOR: *Solander Industries Pty. Ltd.*
LANDSCAPE: *Woodmans Nursery and Landscaping*
INTERIOR DESIGN: *Chhada Siembieda & Associates*

Sheraton Hobart Hotel

LOCATION: *Hobart, Tasmania, Australia*
CLIENT: *Tasmania State Government*
  G.H.D. – Planner West Property, Ltd.
ASSOCIATE ARCHITECT: *Devine Erby Mazli, Australia Pty. Ltd.*
LANDSCAPE: *Landscan Pty. Ltd.*
INTERIOR DESIGN: *Inscan Design Pty. Ltd. Interior Architects*

The Ritz-Carlton, Rancho Mirage

LOCATION: *Rancho Mirage, California*
CLIENT : *Partnership of Federated Development Co./The Ritz-Carlton Hotel Company*
CONTRACTOR: *HCB Contractors, Los Angeles*
LANDSCAPE: *Peridian Group*
INTERIOR DESIGN: *Frank Nicholson, Inc.*

Pacific Islands Club Saipan

LOCATION: *San Antonio, Saipan, C.N. Mariana Islands*
CLIENT: *Inter-Pacific Resorts*
ASSOCIATE ARCHITECT: *Taniguchi-Ruth-Smith & Associates*
CONTRACTOR: *Fletcher Pacific*
LANDSCAPE: *Belt Collins Hawaii/Rock & Waterscape Systems, Inc.*
INTERIOR DESIGN: *Barbara Elliott*
ROCK/WATER WORKS: *Rock & Waterscape Systems, Inc.*

1990

Cheju Shilla Hotel

LOCATION: *Cheju Island, Korea*
CLIENT: *The Shilla Hotel Company (Sam Sung Group)*
ASSOCIATE ARCHITECT: *Sam Woo Architects & Engineers*
CONTRACTOR: *Sam Sung Construction Co., Ltd.*
LANDSCAPE: *Belt Collins Hawaii*
INTERIOR DESIGN: *Ogawa Ferre-Duthillene Decoration*

Four Seasons Resort Wailea

LOCATION: *Wailea, Maui, Hawaii*
CLIENT: *Wailea Beach Palace Company (TSA Development Company, Ltd.)*
CONTRACTOR: *Shimizu Construction Company, Ltd.*
LANDSCAPE: *Walters Kimura & Associates, Inc.*
INTERIOR DESIGN: *James Northcutt Associates*

Goa Renaissance Resort

LOCATION: *Varco Beach, Goa, India*
CLIENT: *Sunder G. Advani*
  Ramada Hotels India
ASSOCIATE ARCHITECT: *Prakash Mankhar & Associates*
CONTRACTOR: *Gharji Eastern Structural and Servicing Engineers*
LANDSCAPE: *Belt Collins Hawaii/Kishore Pradhan*
INTERIOR DESIGN: *Prakash Mankhar & Associates*

1990

The Ritz-Carlton, Marina del Rey

LOCATION: *Marina del Rey, California*
CLIENT: *The Ritz-Carlton Hotel Company*
ASSOCIATE ARCHITECT: *Nathan Evans Pounders & Taylor, Memphis, Tennessee*
CONTRACTOR: *Huntcor Inc.*
LANDSCAPE: *Perry Burr Associates/Peridian Group*
INTERIOR DESIGN: *Frank Nicholson, Inc.*

The Ritz-Carlton, Mauna Lani

LOCATION: *North Kohala Coast, Hawaii*
CLIENT: *The Ritz-Carlton Hotel Company*
CONTRACTOR: *Hawaiian Dredging Construction*
LANDSCAPE: *Peridian Group*
INTERIOR DESIGN: *Frank Nicholson, Inc.*

Waterfront Hilton

LOCATION: *Huntington Beach, California*
CLIENT: *The Robert Mayer Corporation*
CONTRACTOR: *J.A. Jones Construction Co.*
LANDSCAPE: *The SWA Group*
INTERIOR DESIGN: *Concepts 4*
HOTEL CONSULTANT: *James T. Kelly & Associates*

1991

Hyatt Regency Kauai

LOCATION: *Poipu Beach, Kauai, Hawaii*
CLIENT: *Ainako Development Corporation
    Kawailoa Development*
CONTRACTOR: *Hawaiian Dredging Construction*
LANDSCAPE: *Tongg Clarke & Mechler*
INTERIOR DESIGN: *Hirsch-Bedner & Associates*

Aviara Golf Clubhouse & Academy

LOCATION: *Carlsbad, California*
CLIENT: *Aviara Resort Associates*
CONTRACTOR: *Roel Construction Company, Inc., San Diego*
LANDSCAPE: *ONA Landscape Architecture & Planning*
INTERIOR DESIGN: *Wilson & Associates*

Grand Hyatt Bali and Galleria Retail/Cultural Centre

LOCATION: *Nusa Dua, Bali, Indonesia*
CLIENT: *P.T. Wynncor Bali*
ASSOCIATE ARCHITECTS: *Naokazu Hanadoh/Kazubiko Kuroka Architect, International*
CONTRACTOR: *Shimizu Construction Company, Ltd., Tokyo*
LANDSCAPE: *Tongg Clarke & Mechler, Honolulu*
INTERIOR DESIGN: *Hirsch-Bedner & Associates, Hong Kong*

Palm Hills Golf Resort & Spa

LOCATION: *Itoman City, Okinawa, Japan*
CLIENT: *Takakura Corporation*
ASSOCIATE ARCHITECT: *BAU Architects & Associates*
LANDSCAPE: *Tongg Clarke & Mechler*
INTERIOR DESIGN: *Hirsch-Bedner & Associates*
MASTER PLANNING: *Helber Hastert*

The Ritz-Carlton, Amelia Island

LOCATION: *Amelia Island, Jacksonville, Florida*
CLIENT: *The Ritz-Carlton Hotel Company*
ASSOCIATE ARCHITECT: *KBJ Architects, Inc.*
LANDSCAPE: *Peridian Group*
INTERIOR DESIGN: *Frank Nicholson, Inc.*

The Ritz-Carlton Huntington Hotel

LOCATION: *Pasadena, California*
CLIENT: *Huntington Hotel Partners*
ASSOCIATE ARCHITECT: *McClellan, Cruz, Gaylord & Associates, Pasadena*
CONTRACTOR: *Swinerton & Walberg*
LANDSCAPE: *Peridian Group*
INTERIOR DESIGN: *Wilson & Associates*
HISTORIC ARCHITECTURE: *DeBretville and Polyzoids*

The Ritz-Carlton, Palm Beach

LOCATION: *Palm Beach, Florida*
CLIENT: *The Ritz-Carlton Hotel Company*
   Melvin Simon & Associates
ASSOCIATE ARCHITECTS: *Chapman Coyle Chapman & Associates*
LANDSCAPE: *Peridian Group*
INTERIOR DESIGN: *Frank Nicholson, Inc.*

1992 Disneyland© Hotel

LOCATION: *Euro Disneyland© Resort, Marne LaVallée, France*
CLIENT: *Euro Disneyland Corporation*
CONTRACTOR: *Bovis International, Ltd.*
LANDSCAPE: *POD/Sasaki; EDAW, Inc.; Michel Massot*
INTERIOR DESIGN: *JMI Designs Inc.; Pierre-Yves Rochon S.A.*
PRODUCTION ARCHITECT: *Richard Martinet*

Four Seasons Hotel Chinzan-so, Tokyo

LOCATION: *Tokyo, Japan*
CLIENT: *Fujita Tourist Enterprises Company, Ltd.*
ASSOCIATE ARCHITECT: *Yozo Shibata & Associates Architects &*
   Designers, Tokyo, Japan (Kanko Kikaku Sekkeisha)
CONTRACTOR: *Shimizu Construction Company, Ltd.*
LANDSCAPE: *The Dike Partnership*
INTERIOR DESIGN: *Frank Nicholson, Inc.*

1992 *Grand Palazzo Resort*

LOCATION: *St. Thomas, US Virgin Islands*
CLIENT: *Pemberton Resorts*
ASSOCIATE ARCHITECT: *Ian Morrison Architects, Barbados*
CONTRACTOR: *BCM-Cape, Ltd.*
LANDSCAPE: *Stoddart & Tabora*
INTERIOR DESIGN: *The Peter Instan Design Company*

The Lost City

LOCATION: *Republic of Bophuthatswana, South Africa*
CLIENT: *Sun International Ltd.*
ASSOCIATE ARCHITECT: *MV3 Architects, Sandton, South Africa*
CONTRACTOR: *Stocks & Stocks Properties Ltd.*
LANDSCAPE: *Patrick Watson/Top Turf & Associates/ Rock & Waterscape Systems, Inc.*
WATER FEATURES: *Aquatic Design Group, Inc.*

GRAPHICS: *David Carter Graphic Design Associates*
MASTER PLANNING: *Helber Hastert*

The Palace of The Lost City

LOCATION: *Republic of Bophuthatswana, South Africa*
CLIENT: *Sun International Ltd.*
ASSOCIATE ARCHITECT: *Burg Doherty Bryant & Partners, Pretoria, South Africa*
CONTRACTOR: *Stocks & Stocks Properties Ltd.*
LANDSCAPE: *Patrick Watson/Top Turf & Associates/Rock & Waterscape Systems, Inc.*
INTERIOR DESIGN: *Wilson & Associates*

The Ritz-Carlton, Kapalua

LOCATION: *Kapalua, Maui, Hawaii*
CLIENT: *Kaptel Associates*
CONTRACTOR: *Hawaiian Dredging Construction*
LANDSCAPE: *Peridian Group*
INTERIOR DESIGN: *Frank Nicholson, Inc.*

1993 *Principe Felipe, Hyatt La Manga Club*

LOCATION: *Cartagena, Murcia, Spain*
CLIENT: *Bovis Abroad Limited*
ASSOCIATE ARCHITECT: *Jaime J. Bourne & Associates*
CONTRACTOR: *Bovis International Limited*
INTERIOR DESIGN: *Gregory Aeberhard PLC*

The Bluffs at Mauna Kea

LOCATION: *North Kohala Coast, Hawaii*
CLIENT: *Mauna Kea Properties*
CONTRACTOR: *Birtcher/Kikai Joint Venture*
INTERIOR DESIGN: *Merrill & Associates Inc.*

184

Broken Top

LOCATION: *Bend, Oregon*
CLIENT: *Broken Top, Inc.*
CONTRACTOR: *R.D. Olson Construction*
LANDSCAPE: *Peridian Group*
INTERIOR DESIGN: *RCI, Inc., Seattle, Washington*
MASTER PLANNING: *Helber Hastert*

Four Seasons Hotel Mexico City

LOCATION: *Mexico City, Mexico*
CLIENT: *Proparmex S.A. de C.V.*
ASSOCIATE ARCHITECT: *GTM International, France*
CONTRACTOR: *Huartym, S.A. de C.V.*
INTERIOR DESIGN: *InterArt*

Green Villa Hotel

LOCATION: *Cheju Island, Korea*
CLIENT: *Green Villa Corporation*
ASSOCIATE ARCHITECT: *Jung Il*

Hapuna Beach Prince Hotel

LOCATION: *Kohala Coast, Hawaii*
CLIENT: *Mauna Kea Properties Inc.*
CONTRACTOR: *Hawaiian Dredging Construction*
LANDSCAPE: *Belt Collins Hawaii/Sasaki Environmental Design*
INTERIOR DESIGN: *James Northcutt & Associates*

House of Blues

LOCATION: *West Hollywood, California*
CLIENT: *Isaac Tigrett*
CONTRACTOR: *Building Trade Services, San Diego*
LANDSCAPE: *The Dike Partnership*
DEVELOPMENT MANAGER: *C.T. Management, Inc.*

Sheraton Harbor Island Resort (renovation)

LOCATION: *San Diego, California*
CLIENT: *ITT Sheraton Corporation*
CONTRACTOR: *Charles Pankow Builders, Ltd. San Diego*
LANDSCAPE: *Peridian Group*
INTERIOR DESIGN: *Wilson & Associates*
WATER FEATURES: *Sto Design Group*

1994 *Wailea Golf Clubhouse*

LOCATION: *Wailea, Maui, Hawaii*
CLIENT: *Wailea Resort Company Ltd.*
CONTRACTOR: *G.W. Murphy Construction Company*
LANDSCAPE: *Walters Kimura Motoda, Inc.*
INTERIOR DESIGN: *Design Masters, Inc.*
MASTER PLANNING: *Helber Hastert*

1995 *Monte's on Sloane Dining & Entertainment Club*

LOCATION: *London, England*
CLIENT: *Desert Express Ltd.*
CONTRACTOR: *Wallis Ltd. (Kier Group)*
INTERIOR DESIGN & RENDERINGS: *Adam D. Tihany International, Ltd.*
PROJECT MANAGEMENT: *Andrew Young & Co.*

Elgouna Mövenpick Hotel Jolie Ville

LOCATION: *Hurghada, Red Sea, Egypt*
CLIENT: *Orascom Touristic Establishments, Cairo*
ASSOCIATE ARCHITECT: *Orascom, Cairo*
LANDSCAPE: *John Chetham, Adel Niazi Mostafa, Cairo*
INTERIOR DESIGN: *Ibrahim Nagi, Cairo*

Grand Hyatt Cabo del Sol

LOCATION: *Cabo del Sol, Los Cabos, Mexico*
CLIENT: *Quinta del Golfo de Cortez, S.A. de C.V.*
ASSOCIATE ARCHITECTS: *COSA, S.A. de C.V.*
CONTRACTOR: *COSA*
LANDSCAPE: *George W. Girvin Associates*
INTERIOR DESIGN: *A.I. Panamericana, S.C.*
ARCHITECTURAL CHARACTER: *Arthur Valdes Co., Ltd.*

Lanka Oberoi Redevelopment

LOCATION: *Colombo, Sri Lanka*
CLIENT: *Asian Hotels Corporation, Ltd.*
ASSOCIATE ARCHITECT: *Design Consortium Limited*
LANDSCAPE: *Tongg Clarke & Mechler*
INTERIOR DESIGN: *Chhada Siembieda & Associates, Hong Kong*

Paradise Island Resort & Casino

LOCATION: *Nassau, Bahamas*
CLIENT: *Sun International*
ASSOCIATE ARCHITECT: *The Architects Partnership*
CONTRACTOR: *Centex Rooney*
LANDSCAPE: *EDSA–Edward D. Stone, Jr. & Associates*
INTERIOR DESIGN: *Wilson & Associates*
WATER FEATURES: *Aquatic Design Group*
ROCKSCAPE: *Rock & Waterscape Systems, Inc.*

Equatorial Hotel, Bangi

LOCATION: *Kuala Lumpur, Malaysia*
CLIENT: *Bangi Hotel Sdn. Bhd.*
Bangi Resort & Development Corporation Sdn. Bhd.
Arab-Malaysian Leisure Holdings Sdn. Bhd.
Hotel Equatorial (M) Sdn. Bhd.
ASSOCIATE ARCHITECT: *Idris Bhat & Associates, Kuala Lumpur*
INTERIOR DESIGN: *Design One, Los Angeles*

1996 Oak Valley Resort

LOCATION: *Kang-Won-Do, South Korea*
CLIENT/OWNER: *International Resort Corporation*
ASSOCIATE ARCHITECT: *Il Song, Architects & Engineers*
LANDSCAPE ARCHITECT: *Belt Collins Hawaii*
GOLF COURSE ARCHITECT: *Robert Trent Jones II*

LEGO World Family Theme Park

LOCATION: *Windsor, England*
CLIENT: *LEGO World A/S*
LANDSCAPE: *Gillespies*
PROJECT MANAGEMENT/CONSTRUCTION: *Bovis International Ltd.*
ENGINEERING: *Mott MacDonald Group*
ATTRACTIONS: *Ideas (Yorkshire) Ltd./Wyatt Design Associates*
RETAIL INTERIORS: *XMPR International*

Nikko Bali

LOCATION: *Sawangan, Bali, Indonesia*
CLIENT: *Pt. Caterison*
ASSOCIATE ARCHITECT: *Pt. Airmas Asri*
LANDSCAPE: *Peridian Group*
INTERIOR DESIGN: *Barry Design*

Old Town Temecula Entertainment Center

LOCATION: *Temecula, California*
CLIENT: *City Of Temecula & Zev Buffman Group*

1997 Hawai'i Convention Center

LOCATION: *Waikiki, Oahu, Hawaii*
CLIENT: *State of Hawaii*
ASSOCIATE ARCHITECT: *Loschky Marquardt & Nesholm, Seattle*
CONTRACTOR: *Nordic Construction of Honolulu/PCL Construction of Bellevue, WA*

LANDSCAPE: *Walters Kimura Motoda, Inc.*
INTERIOR DESIGN: *Philpotts & Associates, Inc.*
HAWAIIANA CONSULTANTS: *George Kanahele & Associates*

COLLABORATORS

Peer Abben
Renee Abdessalam
Doug Ackerman
John Ackerman
Alberto Acuna
Catherine Adachi
Donald Adams
Ernesto Agaloos, Jr.
Ellen Agcaoili
Peter Aiello
Lois Ajifu
Melvin Ako
Stephen Albert
Wais Karim Ali
Rick Allen
Gerald Allison
Lynn Allison
David Alsop
Lori Ann Amaki
Takahashi Ande
Patrick Andersen
Mary Anderson
Lorrin Andrade
Cecilia Angulo
Charles Apel
Homeyra Arbabi
Storm Archer III
Gretchen Arnemann
Alma Arnold
Rashid Ashraf
Jennifer Asselstine
Charlotte Atkinson
Bunny Au
Nancy Au Kawanouc
William Au
Fely Baisac
Robert Baldino
Pam Baldwin
Ronald Banco
Scott Barbour
Dan Barlev
Lell Barnes
Dee Bartlett
Gilbert Basbas
Michael Batchelor
Luis Beckford
Christopher Belknap
David Bell
Francine Benkovsky
Kristina Benkovsky
Marcia Benson
George Berean
David Berggren

Maureen Bergin
Ruben Betancourt
Josette Bevirt
John Bigay
Randy Bishop
Catherine Blackburn
Carla Bloom
Harold Bock
Boanerges Bolanos
Thanu Boonyawatana
Richard Bosch
Stephen Bossart
Nathalie Boyoro
Cynthia Boyle
Robert Boyle
Nathalie Boyoro
Gordon Bradley
Cary Brockman
Penelope Brocksen
Alex Brostek
Brittney Brown
Dorothy Brown
Perry Brown
Rebecca Brown
Samuel Brown
Victoria Brown
Jerry Browning
Patricia Browning
Michael Brownlie
Cara Brunk
Keith Bryant
Samuel Budiono
Kevin Burt
Bonifacio Butardo
Dale Butler
C.E. Bye
Dedicacion Cabreros
Naidah Cabrido
Susan Cain
Kari Calame
Michael Calame
Bertine Callow
Lucas Camacho
Phillip Camp
Thomas Cannon
Christy Canter
Roberto Caragay
Jennifer Caravalho
Beth Carlson
Bradley Carlson
Tamara Carroll
Samuel Carson
Elise Carter

Oscar Castelo
Cesar Castillo
Monica Caudillo
Curtis Chan
Henry Chang
Spencer Chang
Sidney Char
Robin Chard
Chau-Hsin Chen
Sung-Cheng Chen
Rachel Chesterfield
Norman Cheung
Sharon Ching
Ion Chiose
Nancy Chitwood
Tat (Alex) Cho
Owen Chock
Sunny Choi
Canossa Choy
Mel Choy
David Christensen
Scott Christensen
Carol Chun
Catherine Chun
Kathleen Chun
Kevin Chun
Michael Chun
Terrance Cisco
Jill Claus
Peter Clement
Christine Cline
Keith Cockett
Adam Coghill
Andrea Coghill
Gregory Coghill
G. Cole
David Coloma
Deanna Cone
Marie Connell
Walter Connors
Howard Cook
P. Cook
Meg Corbett
Charles Corwin
Arnel Costa
Mazeppa Costa
Page Costa
Robert Costa
Cheryl Costello
Robert Cox
Cheryl Creber
Virginia Criley
Keith Crockett

Robert Crone
Mildred Crowson
Monica Cuervo
Howard Culbreth II
Fiona Cumming
Lawrence Cunha
David Curry
Sandra Czerniak-Bye
Lizabeth Czerniel
Michael Czoik
David Daniels
Melanie Daniels
Cary Dasenbrock
Leon David
Tom David
Scott Davis
Patrick Dawson
Andrea De Camp
Thomas De Costa
Kathie De Leon
Maurice De Leon
Thomas Deem
Paul Degenkolb
Cida Deguchi
Iluminada Delos
  Santos
Paolo Diaz
J. Ascenzo Digiacomo
David Dike
Rodrigo Dimla
John Dixon
Dimitri Dobrescu
Janice Doering
Robert Dollar
Stephanie Domingo
Gerald Dunn
Jean Dusek Klueter
Jesus Eballar
John Edwards
Karen Eichman
Divina Elefante
John Elliott
Marina Ellison-
  Nyerges
Maggie Emery
Holly Enete
Sherry Eshenbaugh
Raul Espiritu
Elvira Estrada
Ilustre Estrella
Rosauro Eva, Jr.
Manuel Evalle
Anna Marie Evans

Scott Ezer
Bruce Fairweather
Donald Fairweather
Thomas Fee
Leslie Feeney
Gerald Ferguson
Augusto Fernandez
Lori Fernandez
Ruby Fernandez
Bryan Figuered
Krista Findlay
Steve Fischer
Al Fisher
Jean Fisher
Joni Fisher
Thomas Fo
Randall Fong
Lynne Ford
Leilani Fortuno
Lorraine Foster
Robert Fox
Emmanoel Francisco
Mary Ann Frank
Dean Fukawa
Arnold Fukunaga
Jay Fulton
Louis Fulton
Jason Fung
Jeff Feng Gao
Julie Gracia
Howard Garris
Michael Ray Garris
Mary Gaudet
Ursula Gehrmann
Patricia Geminell
Sara Geyer
Robert Gibson
Gary Gidcumb
Patrick Girvin
Lisa Gobeo
Richard Gomez
Cathy Gonzales
Barbara Goo
Debbie-Jaye Goo
Donald Goo
Wayne Goo
John Gould III
James Grady
Renate Granitzer
Andrea Grassi
Frank Gratton
Deeann Gray
Deborah Green

Andreas Grieg
Marjory Griggs
Pamela Gring
Gail Gronau-Brown
William Gulstrom
Mary Haase
Thomas Haeg
Marian Haggerty
Tanya Hagiwara
N. Robert Hale
Craig Hall
Sara Hall
Simeon Halstead
Elaine Han
James Handsel
Cheri Hanna
Edith Hara
Diane Hardie
William Hardman
Ian Harris
Fritz Harris-Glade
Engel Harrop
Horace Hartman
James Harty
Mildred Harvey
Nazie Hashemi
Mark Hastert
Edward Haysom
Gregory Hee
Larry Helber
David Henderson
Pamela Hendrickson
Jeremy Heyes
Betty Hickok
Elizabeth Higa
Jack Highwart
Lois Hiram
Ray Hirohama
Wendy Hisashima
Sheila Hixenbaugh
Kim Hoite
Ronald Holecek
Katherine
    Hollingsworth
Ila Hoopai
Cynthia Hope
Carol Hopkins
James Horman
Charles Horne
Anne Hritzay
Tony Hudziak
M. Hueftle
Bent Huld

Bryant Humann
Mavis Hunnisett
Harry Hunt
Brian Husting
Susan Ings
Arkanit Intarajit
Puangthong Intarajit
Robert Iopa
Ra'ana Islam
Rafique Islam
Cynthia Jacobs
Joseph Jacobs
Ruben Jaictin
Tammy James
Cristina Janigan
Kenneth Jenkins
Dae Soo Ji
Francis Johnson
James Johnson
Jennifer Johnson
Jon Johnson
Lon Johnson
Lynne Johnson
Michael Johnson
Nilda Johnson
Paul Jones
Natalia Juliano
Carole Kajiwara
Kenneth Kajiwara
Christine Kakour
Shirley Kanahele
Laura Kanazawa
Daniel Kanekuni
Anne Kanemoto
Denise Kaneshiro
Jason Kaneshiro
William Kanotz
Stephanie Kapanui
Judith Kaplan
Barry Karim
Milan Karlovac
Mark Kasarjian
Stanley Kawasaki
Steven Kearns
Reyna Keaunui
Rosemary Keefe
Nicky Kelly
Kathleen Kelm
Nils Kenaston
Kelley Kesinger
Gregory Kessler
Sunchai Keuysuvan
Francik Khalili

Rumman Khan
Ashley Kim
Dennis Kim
Naomi Kim
Glenn Kimura
Lucille Kimura
Robert Kleinkopf
Chris Knight
Hideo Kobayashi
Laureen Kodama
Jan J. Kofranek
Marcella Kofranek
Justin Koizumi
Ellery Komenaka
Olivier Koning
Richard Koob
Karl Korth
Koizumi Kotaro
George Koteles
Mikako Koyama
Connie Kruayai
Stanley Kruse
Collen Kunishige
Caroline Kuo
Leslie Kurasaki
Ronald Kwan
Henry Kwok
Joan LaFountaine
Amy Lam
Clemson Lam
Sharon Lang
James Langan
Robert Larsen
Ingrig Larsson
Charles Lau
Elena Lau
John Lau
Marianne Lau
J. Patrick Lawrence
C. Lawson
Leonilo Laxa
Leslie LeBon
Anna Lee
Bernard Lee
Chang Lee
Darren Lee
Donald Lee
Edna Lee
Gray Lee
Hideko Tanaka Lee
Joann Lee
Yo Han Lee
Pedrito Leong

John Leopardi
Karen Levesque
Feliciano Libao
Bob Liebsack
Lori Liermann
Thomas Lim
John David Lindsay
Tom Litaker
Romela Lloren
Christopher Lloyd
James Loft
Harold Lopez
Daniel Loriot
Jose Luciano
John Ludlow
Herb Luke
Sherilyn Lum
Kyle Lung
Nilo Mabunay
Deborah Mace
Marica Mack
Lynden Mackawa
Ross Mackenzie
Maureen MacKinnon
Jeffrey MacNeil
Maureen Madigan
R. Maeda
Keith Maekawa
Robby Mago
Edgargo Mallari
Thomas Manok
Mohamed Mansour
Rocky Marquez
Cynthia Marr
Eduardo Martinez
F. Marvin
Eric Matsumoto
Toshiko Matsushita
Robert Mattox
R. Mau
Ross Maxwell
Stephanie May
Fayez Mazid
Richard McAllister
Roberta McCabe
Greg McCants
J. Marie McCormick
Martha McCullough
Victoria McDonald
Mirjana McGregor
Diane McLeod
Rueko McNally
Bradford McNamee

John McQuown
Karen Mead
Vicki Meece
Louise Mellish
Shirley Mercado
Caralyn Merrill
Elaine Metler
B. Meyers
Lauren Michioka
Svetlana Micic
John Miesen
Fred Mikawa
Vicki Millard
Karen Miller
Michael Milo, Jr.
Peggy Minger-
    McCants
Mohamed Mirza
Linda Mitchell
Ronald Mitchell
Gary Miyakawa
Carrie Miyasato
Janice Miyoshi-
    Vitarelli
Sharon Mizuno
Dale Moen
Susan Moises
D. Molegraaf
Hoover Monleon
Frank Montillo
David Moore
James Moore
Brenda Moors
Ernesto Morales
Susan Morgan
Steven Morita
Adam Morris
Douglas Morris
Jafar Mosleh
Bruce Mosteller
Marie Mundheim
Alan Murakami
Grant Murakami
Craig Murayama
Virginia Murison
Judy Murphy
James Murray
Michelle Musada
Richard Myers
Clint Nagata
Jann Nagato
Ronald Nakagawa
Stephen Nakamitsu

Jeffrey Nakamura
Liane Nakamura
William Nakayama
John Naleyanko
Nadi Nammar
Sally Nava
Stephen Nemeth
Deepak Neupane
Jennifer Neupane
Son Nguyen
Amauri Nicasio
Paul Niiyama
Darrell Nilles
Nancy Nishikawa
Robin Nishimura
Timothy Nomer
Darryl Nordstrom
Andrew Nyerges
Homer Oatman
Laura Oatman
Carol Ann Ogata
Alma O'Hanlon
Jean Olvey
Dawn Onaga
Christine Optiz
Merrilee Orcutt
Katherine Orthman
Ernest Oshiro
Scott Osterhage
Scott Ostrowski
Lori Ournaye
Gilbert Oviedo
Linda Owens
Alison Pace
Emily Pagliaro
Perla Palombo
Michael Paneri
Tina Paneri
Carrie Pannick-Reyes
James Park
John Park
Deborah Parks
N. Parnes
Mark Paskill
Ramesh Patel
Geoff Patterson
E. Duff Paulsen
Robert Payan
Bernard Pebenito
Anne Perez
M. Perry
Christine Pesce
Jon Pharis

Richard Phillips
Apinant Phuphatana
Andrea Piper
Udom Pongsawat
Susan Poole
Allan Porter
Azita Pourmehr
Nick Poynton
Darmawan
Prawirohardjo
Brian Prock
Shirley Pyun
Manolo Quiason
Teresa Quincey
Suzanne Rabey
Kay Radzik
Anthony Ramirez
Mariano Ramirez
Carl Ramos
Vikki Raschbacher
Scott Redfield
Emma Redor
William Reed
Art Reola
Heather Reynolds
Nicholas Reynolds
Nathaneal Richards
Sarah Richardson
Carol Rieck
Paul Ries
Daniel Riordan
Andre Riou
Barry Robinson
Eduardo Robles
Victor Robles
Larry Rocha
Kimberly Rodrigues
Gabriel Rodriguez
J. Lee Rofkind
Elizabeth Rosas
Michael Rosen
Katherine Rothrock
Donal Rounds
Rosemary Rowan
Pamela Rudin
Prudencio Rumbaoa
Patrick Russel
Thomas Russell
Lila Ruzicka
Helen Ryan
Edie Sagarang
Tatsuo Saito
Wendell Sakagawa

Gregorio Salinas, Jr.
Richard Salvato
Reynaldo Santos
Dennis Sapphire
Atilano Saradpon
Daniel Sauerbrey
Marios Savopoulos
Robert Schaeffer
Dorothy Schafer
Anna Schef
Thomas Schmidt
James Schmit
Kevin Scholl
Peter Scott
Patti Seay
Lydia Seeley
Peter Seo
Yosesh Seth
Beth Shafer
Pankaj Shah
Leslie Shammas
Ali Shams
Donald Shaw
Ralph Shelbourne
Han Shi
Vincent Shigekuni
John Shigenaga
Colin Shimokawa
Janine Shinoki
David Shu
Eduardo Silva
Jennifer Silva
Charles Sims
Crispolo Sindiong
B. Skadsheim
Thomas Smail
Darren Smith
Eric Smith
Lisa Smith
Valentine Snell
Thomas Snodgrass
Mitzi Snyder
Norman Soohoo
Brian Spahr
Robert Stempner
Jan Stenberg
Angelica Stern
Robert Stern
Sandy Stern
Cindy Stewart
Amy Stillman
Timothy Stoaks
Stella Stojik

Ivory Chris Stokes
Audrey Strapple
L. Strauss
Martin Stuart
Karl Stumpf
Lloyd Sueda
Karen Suenaga
David Sung
Patrick Sutton
Robert Sutton
Douglas Swank
Arlyn Sweesy
Glenn Sweesy
Garrett Tagawa
Elissa Tajon
Stanley Takaki
Gerald Tanako
Dorene Takenaka
Joni Takenaka
Serenity Talbot
Joyce Tamanaha
Keith Tamura
Vince Tamura
Xiaosi Tan
Dennis Tarampi
Susan Tasaki
Mark Tawara
Thomas Tengan
Evelyn Tenorio
Alan Teoh
Nestor Terrill
Cliff Terry
Clark Thiel
John Steffan Thiersch
James Thomassen
Mark Thomassen
Ann Thompson
Robert Tindall
Henry Ting
Lisa Tokumaru
Sharie Tokumoto
G. Tokuno
Joann Toledo
Gregory Tong
Reynaldo Torres
Randy Totel
Lisa Troke
Shirly Tsang
Sean Tully
Ismet Turkalp
Anglier Turner
Terry Tusher
Alexander Uahihui

Yurica Ueda
Benjamin Ugale
Lex Ulibarri
E. Umemoto
Robert Umemura
Jeanne Ung
Susan Uno
Ronald Uyesugi
Gail Uyetake
Farrokh Vahid
Holly Valentine-
Steinhoff
Jason Van Auker
Cheryl Ann Van
Berkel
Richard Van Horn
Ronald Van Pelt
Lisa Varela
John Vargas
Joaquin Vasquez
Rafael Velazquez
Valerie Velves
Brian Veneble
Marc Ventura
Jon Veregge
Carol Vesco
Rudolfo Victorio
Ricardo Viernes
Roberto Viggayan
Marcia Villegins
Tracy Vincent
Mark Vogt
Deirdre Vouziers
Jolie Wah
Jennifer Wakazuru
Kimberly Walker
Charles Wallace
Thomas Walsh
Mark Walter
George Walters
Marcy Wang
Cindy Wasserman
Eugene Watanabe
Linda Watanabe
Douglas Waterman
Leslie Watson
Alisa Weaver
Marion Weeber
John Weitz
Robert Wenkham
Amy Wert
George Whisenand
Loy Whisenand

Sabine White
Mark Whitehouse
Michelle Willey
Eugene Williams
Michael Williams
Soh-Hyon Wilson
Suzanne Wilson
George J. "Pete"
Wimberly
Heather Wimberly
Tom Witaker
Howard Wolff
Willard Won
Flora Wong
Miranda Wong
Robert Wong
Stanley Wong
David Woo
Steven Worthington
Michelle Gina Wright
Henry Thanh Wu
Thelma Wurm
Charles Wyse
Kurt Xu
Jennifer Yagi
Clarice Yamada
Ross Yamamoto
Roy Yamamoto
Corinne Yamasaki
Brett Yamashita
Chew Leng Yap
Ross Yokoyama
Kevin Yoneda
Robert Yonooka
Kellie Yost
Nancy Yost
Allison Young
Kevin Young
Lawrence Young
Richard Young
Donna Yuen
Sorin Zdrahal
Donald Ziebell
Kelly Ziegler
Hongliang Zou

ABOUT THE AUTHORS

RAY BRADBURY is one of the most prolific and best-selling writers of the 20th century, with classics such as *Fahrenheit 451, Dandelion Wine, The Illustrated Man,* and *The Martian Chronicles* to his credit. Through his novels, short stories, poems, operas, musicals, and screenplays, and through his design contributions to theme parks, shopping centers, and entire cities, Mr. Bradbury continues to create the future.

JOHN NAISBITT is one of the world's leading trend forecasters, who annually speaks to thousands of business leaders and opinion makers in the Americas, Europe, and Asia. Mr. Naisbitt's sixth book, *Global Paradox,* applies a single conceptual breakthrough to seemingly disparate trends. His previous book about the global future was *Megatrends 2000,* an international bestseller.

MICHAEL S. RUBIN, PH.D., is president of MRA International, a consulting firm specializing in creative programming and strategy implementation for the leisure, entertainment, and real estate development industries. Dr. Rubin received his doctorate from the Wharton School of Finance and his architecture degree from the University of Pennsylvania, where he continues to serve on the faculty.

If words were buildings, MAZEPPA KING COSTA would be a prominent architect. She has built many, many stories in the course of her productive and illustrious career writing for the design industry.

A prolific author and award-winning playwright, BETH CRAWFORD VINCENT is as comfortable writing about palaces in Africa as she is writing about juke joints in Mississippi. Her work has appeared in over 100 international publications.

Having worked with architects from Maui to Massachusetts, JANA WOLFF has written for and about design professionals for over 20 years. A published author who is most often a ghostwriter, she produces volumes of work under other people's bylines.

INDEX OF PHOTOGRAPHERS

FRONT COVER

Hotel Bora Bora
Douglas Peebles

The Palace of
The Lost City
Courtesy of Sun International

BACK COVER

Disney's® Grand Floridian Beach Resort
Courtesy of Disney Development Company

The Ritz-Carlton, Laguna Niguel
Milroy & McAleer

Hyatt Regency Kauai
Milroy & McAleer

GLOBALIZATION OF THE WORLD'S LARGEST INDUSTRY

Courtesy of Sun International (p8)

THE ANATOMY OF A DESTINATION

*Douglas Peebles (p10)
Milroy & McAleer (p11)
Robert Miller (p12)
Courtesy of Sun International (p13)*

HOSPITALITY PROJECTS

Courtesy of Sun International (p15)

Hotel Bora Bora
Douglas Peebles

Ramada Great Barrier Reef Resort
*John Ivanovic, Studio One
David Franzen (p20)*

Four Seasons Hotel Mexico City
Robert Miller

The Ritz-Carlton, Naples
Milroy & McAleer

Hyatt Regency Kauai
*Milroy & McAleer
Olivier Koning (p30, left; p32, bottom-right)
Courtesy of Hyatt Regency Kauai (p32, top)
Howard Wolff (p34, top-left and bottom-left)
WAT&G (p30, right)*

Shangri-La Hotel, Garden Wing
David Franzen

Hyatt Regency Cheju
*Kyle Rothenborg
Courtesy of Hyatt Regency Cheju (p41; p42)
WAT&G (p40)*

The Ritz-Carlton, Rancho Mirage
Berger/Conser

Grand Palazzo Resort
Bruce Stanford

The Ritz-Carlton, Kapalua
*Howard Wolff
Donna Day (p52 top)
Michael French (p50; p51)*

Goa Renaissance Resort
*Kyle Rothenborg
Courtesy of Goa Renaissance Resort (p55)*

Four Seasons Resort Wailea
*Michael French
Jaime Ardiles-Arce (p57 bottom; p58)
David Franzen (p56)*

The Ritz-Carlton Huntington Hotel
Milroy & McAleer

The Regent of Bangkok
*Courtesy of The Regent of Bangkok
David Franzen (p68 top-left and middle-left)
Kyle Rothenborg (p67; p69 bottom-right)*

Four Seasons Hotel Newport Beach
*Jaime Ardiles-Arce
Ronald Moore & Associates (p72; p73)*

The Ritz-Carlton, Laguna Niguel
Milroy & McAleer

The Palace of
The Lost City
*Courtesy of Sun International
WAT&G (p80; p83 bottom; p84)*

Cheju Shilla Hotel
*Courtesy of Cheju Shilla Hotel
Kyle Rothenborg (p88)*

Sheraton Harbor Island Resort (renovation)
Berger/Conser

Four Seasons Hotel Chinzan-so, Tokyo
Robert Miller

Hyatt Regency Waikiki
*Michael French
Douglas Peebles (p96 bottom)*

The Ritz-Carlton, Mauna Lani
*Milroy & McAleer
Douglas Peebles (p99)*

LEISURE PROJECTS

WAT&G (p103)

Broken Top
Laurie Black

Parkroyal Shopping Village, Cairns International
*Willem Rethmeier
Howard Wolff (p110)*

Principe Felipe, Hyatt La Manga Club
Robert Miller

191